COMMERCIAL
AVIATION
C O L L E C T I B L E S

COMMERCIAL
AVIATION
C O L L E C T I B L E S

AN ILLUSTRATED PRICE GUIDE

RICHARD R. WALLIN

Wallace-Homestead Book Company
Radnor, Pennsylvania

Designed by Anthony Jacobson
Manufactured in the United States of America

Library of Congress Cataloging in Publication Data
Wallin, Richard R.
    Commercial aviation collectibles / Richard R. Wallin.
      p. cm.
   ISBN 0-87069-546-0
   1. Aeronautics, Commercial—Collectibles. I. Title.
TL506.A1W35   1990
629.133'340423'075—dc20   89-51559
                                      CIP

2 3 4 5 6 7 8 9 0   9 8 7 6 5 4 3 2 1

To
my wife, Lorine, for her help and encouragement on
this project, but even more so for her patience with all
these crazy hobbies over the years.

Contents

Preface

This book is intended to provide a ready reference to those items associated with worldwide commercial aviation. With minor exceptions, the scope of collectibles is limited to items used by, issued by, or made for commercial airlines and/or their employees or representatives.

The large display model planes made for the airlines and used for advertising in travel agencies, will be included; other model planes will not. Likewise, while military collectibles is a popular hobby, it is beyond the scope of this volume.

Although, as a price guide, this volume implies that it will be used for commercial purposes by buyers and sellers, I hope that the wide variety of items included will also render it valuable from an educational and entertainment standpoint.

I wish to thank the many individuals who have given support and encouragement to my endeavors in the collecting of airline items, and ultimately the creation of this volume. The kind and willing assistance of R. E. G. Davies was especially appreciated. Davies, the Curator of Air Transport at the Smithsonian National Air and Space Museum, is undoubtedly the world's foremost authority on commercial airline history. The scope of items covered and illustrated in this volume are in a great part due to the help of Shirley and Larry Ibsen and John R. Joiner, who graciously made their collections and personal expertise available to me. Others who freely assisted, in alphabetical order, include Alan Altman, Keith Armes, Stanley Baumwald, Avery Burack, Hector Cabezas, Fred Chan, Paul Collins, John Dekker, Barbara Freeman, Philip Glatt, Earl Godfrey, Albert Goshman, George Hamlin, Richard Luckin, Charles Miller, Bryant Petit, Charles Quarles, Larry Richards, Charles and Mary Ann Schneber, Jon Simmonds, and Hal Turin. Thanks also goes to Brian Matsumoto for working his photographic magic, both behind the camera and in the darkroom. (Items pictured in this volume are from the collection of the author, unless otherwise noted.)

Ironically, as a longtime railroadiana collector, I became interested in airline items through the "back door" by the encouragement of one J. David Ingles, now the editor of *Trains* magazine. First it was playing cards, then glassware, china, timetables, and wings; and soon I found myself at least dabbling in just about every size, shape, and type of collectible associated with commercial aviation. I hope that this book will whet the enthusiasm of the reader to do likewise.

COMMERCIAL
AVIATION
COLLECTIBLES

1 Background

Airline collectibles is a field which has only in the past few years become recognized by dealers of collectibles. One can hardly call even the oldest airline items "antiques" since the traditional definition of an antique is something 100 years old or more (although many "younger" items of all kinds have been assuming that label in recent years). It's been only about 85 years since the Wright brothers first took flight, but it was yet another 25 years before even a primitive semblance of an air transport system emerged.

The *Official Aviation Guide's* first issue, published in February 1929, needed only 15 pages to list all the officers and to show the route maps and schedules of the country's airlines. Interestingly, Continental, Pan Am, and Braniff are the only names from the first issue that still exist today under essentially the same banner. In 1929, as an example, Braniff operated only an Oklahoma City–Tulsa route, using the name Paul R. Braniff, Inc., and its fleet was listed as "1 Stinson Monoplane, 1 Ryan Monoplane."

With today's fleets of several hundred jets for the larger airlines, it is difficult to comprehend just what has happened in the past half century. At 52 years old I find it incredible that as late as two years prior to the year I was born Eastern Airlines was still using an open-cockpit mail plane!

One must keep in mind that the early airlines came into being for a sole purpose—to carry the mail. Passenger service developed more or less as an afterthought. A reading of the early histories of many airlines leaves serious doubt as to whether a profit could ever have been made had the early airlines carried passengers alone. The first lines, at least those which survived, lived and died on the possession of mail contracts, at that time often a political proposition.

Just as the early lines were getting started, the Great Depression hit, and were it not for the government airmail subsidy, all probably would have perished quickly. At that time, the only thing airlines could offer was speed, but the "time is money" concept had not yet come into vogue; the nation's well-developed rail passenger system served the needs of all but the most affluent and adventurous travelers.

The airlines soon realized that an emphasis on service and safety would help increase their passenger revenue. In the early 1930s, the airlines were beginning to realize that the idea of passengers for profit was an attainable goal. Just how or who conceived the idea is unknown, but from the very early days, meals and beverages were served free to airline passengers. Although the bill of fare couldn't come close to that offered in railroad dining cars, it was nevertheless free, a pleasant alternative to often outrageous railroad dining car prices. Colonial Air Transport's June 1, 1929 timetable gives a very early example: "Cabin-steward service, including morning boullion and afternoon tea provided en route, make for extra comfort and enjoyment." What is left unsaid is that the early cabin stewards were usually the copilots, who removed their uniform cap and put on a waiter's vest, becoming an instant primitive example of what we today call a flight attendant.

It is not my intention to document the history of commercial air travel in this volume, but I hope that the preceding paragraphs set the stage for the rarity of some of the few and early airline collectibles from that era, items such as timetables, advertising folders, some early dining service pieces, perhaps a few playing cards, and, of course, the crew wings and badges. Not that much different from what we save from today's carriers, you say? Yes, but the difference is in the numbers. Even as late as 1941, Continental had only six planes and Delta had only nine, and those planes held only a handful of passengers, not the hundreds that today's craft carry.

In the airline collectible field, many collectors focus their field of interest on this or that airline, while others seek anything from a certain type of plane, the DC-3 and Lockheed Constellation being two popular examples. The flying boat category holds almost a cult fascination among many collectors.

Following is a list of airlines commonly referred to by initials, so you can tell at a glance which one is cited.

BAL	Belize Airways Limited
BOAC	British Overseas Airways Corporation
CAAC	Civil Air Administration of China
C&S	Chicago and Southern
CSA	Ceskoslovenske Aerolinie (Czechoslovak Airlines)
JAT	Jugoslovenski Aerotransport (YugoslavAirtransport)
KLM	Royal Dutch Airlines
LOT	Polskie Linie Lotnicze (Polish Airlines)
MAS	Malaysian Airline System
PBA	Provincetown-Boston Airlines
SAS	Scandinavian Airlines System
TAROM	Transporturile Aeriene Romane (Romanian Airlines)
TAT	Transcontinental Air Transport
TWA	Trans World Airlines

2 General In-flight Items

In this chapter we will deal with general items not covered in other chapters which are used on board the plane for the use, convenience, and safety of passengers. As we will see, some of these items are still seen on today's craft, while others are relics of the past.

Safety Cards

Safety cards are plastic laminated cardboard folders, usually about $8\frac{1}{2}''$ × 11″ in size and four pages long, which give information to passengers as to the location of emergency exits on the particular type of plane on which they are flying. Typically these show the exact model of plane, such as 727-231; the airline's name and/or logo; and sometimes a nice color photo of the plane in flight. Collectors value a safety card that is from a plane type no longer operated by the airline for which it is marked. Some collectors try to obtain cards for all of the different plane models operated by a particular airline, while others try to get cards for every airline that ever operated a certain model of plane. Most are valued at $1–$3; rare specimens, $5–$10.

Seat-occupied Cards

Seat-occupied cards are plastic laminated cards, about 4″ × 12″, which were available for use on multi-stop flights. Passengers wanting to make a short visit to the airport between flight segments could leave these cards on their seats. With the advent of the hub-and-spoke flight concept, non-stop flights have become more common and these cards are seldom seen. Usually these cards display the airline name and logo, sometimes in another language on the reverse side. Most are valued at $1–$3; if from a long-gone airline, $5–$10.

Airsickness Bags

Airsickness bags need no description, but despite their unpleasant use, they are collected. Some airlines use only generic bags which have no

3

value, but those marked with an airline name and/or logo are valuable. One fellow from the Netherlands claims to have the world's largest collection of airline "barf bags," nearly 2,000 different kinds. Most are valued at $1–$2.

Headrest Covers

Headrest covers, which are usually cloth but sometimes plastic, are placed on the top of the seats to protect seats from hair oil. They are seldom seen now. Nice examples have the airline name and/or logo prominently shown. Most are valued at $2–$5; extra-nice with old logo or name, $10–$15.

Miniature Soap Bars

Miniature soap bars are found in the restrooms of all planes. Nearly all airlines still use soap wrapped in paper displaying the airline name and logo. These are an attractive, low-cost collectible, and many are readily available showing old names and/or logos. Although these are generally low-ticket items, I must confess to paying $20 for a 1929-era bar showing a TAT trimotor and advertising the short-lived, combined air-rail coast-to-coast service. Most are valued at 25¢–$1.

In-flight Magazines

Issued by virtually all airlines for in-flight reading, in-flight magazines usually feature travel articles on destinations served by the airline. These magazines are usually of minimal value, but some have nice articles on the history of the airline or show pictures of older planes. Most are valued at 25¢–$1.

Amenities Kits

Amenities kits are small kits about the size of a cigar box, usually vinyl (occasionally leather), showing the airline name and/or logo. Most airlines still give these kits out to first class passengers on long international flights. These kits typically include toothbrush, toothpaste, razor, shaving cream, shampoo, shoehorn, nail file, skin cream, ear plugs, eyeshades, cloth slippers, and other similar items that come in handy on a long flight. Most are valued at $5–$15, depending on size, fabric, and contents.

Seat-back Packets

A relic of the days past, these interesting folders are a much-sought collectible. Usually about 6″×12″ and opening into three compartments, these heavy paper folders were designed primarily to inform first-time travelers; they were used by most airlines from the 1940s to the early 1960s. Typically they included a route map, a timetable, a few postcards, airline stationery and envelopes, baggage stickers, and a folder showing the features about the type of airplane on which the passenger was flying. The covers of some packets have a nice color picture of a plane in flight. Most are valued at $25–$50.

Junior Wings

Often nicknamed "kiddie" wings, these small wings are still given by most airlines to children on flights to pin on their clothes. Most often they are a small replica of the wings worn by the cockpit crew and flight attendants on that airline. As with most things in life, these were made of metal until the 1960s, at which time the switch was made to plastic. Most bear some kind of lettering, such as "Junior Pilot" or "Future Pilot." A very popular collectible, these can be obtained free for the asking on most flights. A sizable display of these attractive items are attainable at minimal cost. Most plastic types cost 25¢–$3; common metal varieties go for $3–$5. Older metal styles may be worth up to $35, but many are in the $10 range.

Other Junior Items

To identify minors traveling alone, most airlines have them wear a special unattended-minor button, about 2″ in diameter, with the airline initials and bright striping (value: about $1). For a short period, American Airlines issued small metal rings instead of junior wings. These had the AA eagle logo circled by the "Junior Pilot" wording and had adjustable bands to fit small fingers (value: about $10). A few airlines briefly issued small cloth and plastic replicas of a pilot's cap to young passengers. These had a patch with the airline's name and logo on the front. Most of these caps are valued at $10–$25.

Ozark safety manual. **$3**

Seat-back packet cover from Linea Aeorpostal Venezolana (LAV); 1950s. Cover alone carries **$10** value because of a nice photo of Constellation aircraft on an obscure airline.

Three recent examples of safety cards, valued at about **$2** each. Although these safety cards are not very old (from mid-1980s), PSA has since been merged into USAir, Ozark into TWA, and Aeromexico is going from government to private ownership and may change its name.

Three 1970s safety cards: USAir, **$2;** Frontier Airlines, which went out of business in 1986, **$4;** and Air Illinois, **$5.** The Air Illinois plane pictured crashed in 1983; the airline went out of business in 1984.

Three United safety cards from the 1970s; two have color photos on the covers. **$3** each

Pan Am storybook for young passengers. **$3**

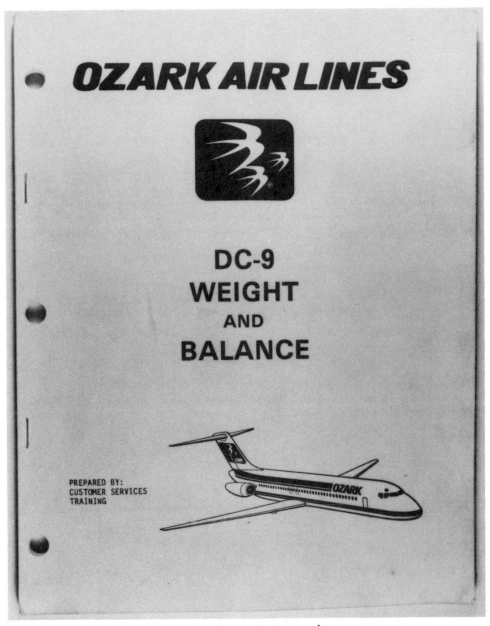

Looseleaf crew manual on DC-9 weight and balance. **$3**

Ticket jackets from about 1980; **$2** each. All companies shown are out of business or have changed their name.

Various designs of kiddie wings from TWA and Ozark; although some look identical, each is different. Recent metal types (left center and bottom three on right), **$4** each; old metal TWA with Indian head (top center), **$25;** remainder are plastic, **$1** each.

American Airlines kiddie rings, Junior Pilot, and Junior Stewardess versions. **$10** each

Unattended-minor button. **$1**

A piece of carpeting from the front passenger compartment bulkhead; Western Airlines, red and black logo on gray background; an unusual item; **$25.** (From the John R. Joiner collection.)

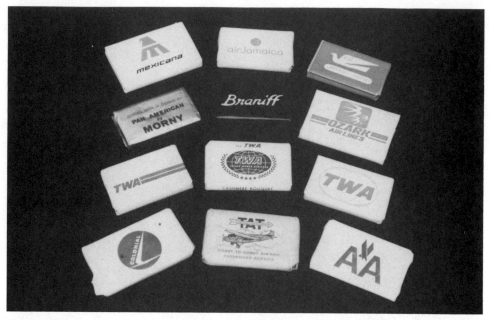

On-board soap bars from various eras. Recent examples, **50¢** each; bar from Colonial (lower left), which merged into Eastern in 1956, **$4;** TAT bar (bottom center) from 1929, **$20.**

Headrest covers. Air Jamaica, cloth, **$3;** American, from the 1970s, heavy vinyl, **$4.**

Seat-occupied cards from the 1970s. **$2** each

TWA seat-back packets, 1950s. **$25** each

In-flight magazines. **$1** each

American seat-back packet with large DC-7 color picture on the cover, 1954. **$35**

Two plastic seat-occupied cards; the Belize (BAL) card is especially nice because the aircraft is pictured in color and because BAL was a very small airline and is no longer in existence. **$3** each

Two early junior wings, from the 1930s; **$30–$35** each. (From the John R. Joiner collection.)

Two tin foil junior wings. Although cheaply made, these were apparently distributed for only a short time; since few have survived, they are rare. **$20–$25** each

Many of the metal wings were on a backing card when issued. This wing on the original card is worth **$10.** (From the John R. Joiner collection.)

Examples of two junior pilot caps. **$20** each

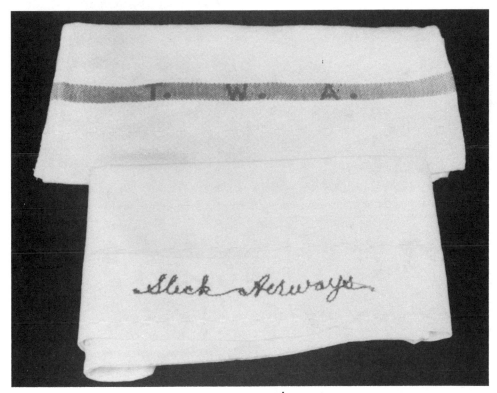

TWA hand towel and Slick Airways pillow case. **$5** each

Bilingual "barf bags" from Mexico's two large airlines. **$1** each

On-board blanket, nicely marked with airline name and logo. **$25**

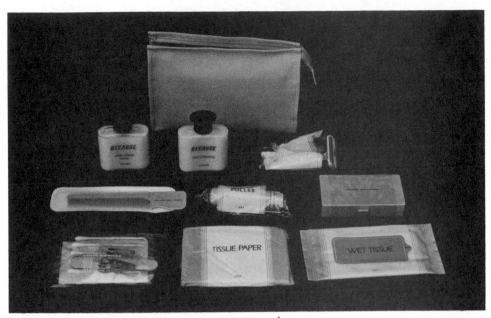

Japan Air Lines amenities kit, showing contents. **$5**

3 China and Dishes

One of the fastest growing segments of airline collectibles is dining service items in general, china in particular.

Airline china is generally attractive, much of it is fine-quality ware, and it is relatively easy to find and collect. Although we tend to think airline china is a thing of the past, nothing could be further from the truth. Today (worldwide) there are between 125 and 150 different airlines which offer first class and/or business class service and serve meals on china. Some even use a different china pattern for each class. As an example, Brazil's Varig Airlines uses china even in the economy section.

Airline food service started with just coffee, juice, and soup, but starting about 1930 complete meals were served on some of the larger lines, such as American, TWA, and United. Planes of that era had no galleys; therefore, items served had to be heated or cooled ahead of time and stored in insulated containers during the flight. During this era, it was common to find china and an early version of plastic (called Bakelite) used together.

Early examples of airline china were made by prominent domestic china manufacturers such as Hall, Homer Laughlin, and Syracuse. Generally, early china was of a lightweight design, since weight was a critical factor in the early days of flying. Shortly after World War II, Syracuse developed a very delicate china called Airlite for American Airlines. There were three pieces in the set: a vegetable dish, a medium plate, and a coffee cup. The latter two had the AA eagle logo (with the eagle facing left) surrounded by stars, all in a light blue color. These are very desirable collectibles, with the cup valued at $50 and the plate at $100.

Until the late 1950s, virtually all airline passengers were accommodated in what might be considered first class, because almost all travelers fell into one of two categories: either businessmen on expense accounts or wealthy leisure passengers. But as planes became larger, it was necessary to attract more people in order to fill the seats, and thus the economy fare was conceived. As we know today, following deregulation, the great majority of passengers are on discount fares which place them in the coach section of the plane. The business and wealthy passengers still fly in first class, which occupies a very small section on most planes.

Due to the wide price gap between first class fares and discounted coach fares, many airlines have offered a business class on widebody planes in recent years. Most airlines use the same china for both first and business classes, while a few, such as British Airways and Malaysian Airlines System, have separate patterns for each. The point is that in past years everyone on planes ate on china, but planes were fewer and smaller in those days.

China was used even into the 1970s by a few airlines which offered only one class of service (coach) but advertised a premium level of that service. Frontier Airlines is a good example. After the Deregulation Act of 1978, there were also a small number of lines formed which offered all first class service. Their selling points were additional legroom, premium meal service, and complimentary cocktails, all at full-coach fares. Among these were McClain, Air One, Air Atlanta, and Midwest Express. For the most part these carriers were undercapitalized, and lasted only a few months, with Midwest Express being the sole survivor.

In a class by itself was Regent Air, which lasted only a couple of years and was probably the most luxurious airline ever. Regent Air operated three 727s configured for 35 seats in both open and private seating arrangements. Gourmet meals were served, and a barber shop was on board, as well as a business secretary. You were shuttled between your home or office and the airport by limousine or helicopter. Regent used fine English Spode china, which is very desirable, collectible, and scarce (value per piece: $25–$100).

China has shown up from some of the least likely carriers. Famous no-frills Laker Airlines of England used Wedgwood china, and the short-lived low-fare Highland Express of Scotland used Royal Doulton.

Today's airline china is manufactured by a list of companies that sounds like a "Who's Who" of fine dinnerware: Rosenthal, Spode, Wedgwood, Royal Doulton, Noritake, etc.

When determining the value of airline china, there are several factors which must be considered. How old is the china? How big is/was the airline? How long was the pattern used? Is the china pattern attractive? China with an attractive design pattern, plus the airline name and/or logo visible on the top or side, is definitely a good collectible.

Among the commonly-found dishes today are the casserole-style pieces still used by most airlines for hot meals in coach class. These are usually about 5″ × 7″ and rectangular with rounded corners. Often made by Corning, Abco, or Pfaltzgraff, these have the airline name impressed or raised on the bottom. Such pieces currently have very little value. A Pfaltzgraff outlet store near Chicago recently had hundreds of these, with the bottoms marked for United Airlines, offered at 25¢ each. Reports indicate that other Pfaltzgraff locations have similar pieces for both American and United with colored flowers painted on the top to entice would-be buyers to these otherwise-plain pieces.

One must be careful of situations in which a sizable airline has changed china patterns or has been involved in a merger. In the 1970s, Delta discontinued using a white china with the airline's red and blue wedge logo on top. Delta's stock of these pieces, which apparently numbered in the thousands, was sold to dealers who advertised it in the *Antique Trader* newspaper. These pieces, the most common of all airline china, can be found frequently at flea markets throughout the country. TWA likewise sold its Royal Ambassador china to the secondary market making it quite common as well. However, since it is considered a very attractive china pattern, and it is manufactured by Rosenthal of Germany, it remains a popular item, and still brings a moderate price ($10–$15 each for plates, bowls and cup and saucer sets). British Airways recently discontinued the china it had used in first class (gold BA crest) and Concorde service (blue and yellow). These are fine Royal Doulton chinas, but a substantial quantity of both sets has appeared on the market recently, making them affordable. The gold crest pieces are valued at about $5 each, and the blue and yellow Concorde pieces are valued at $10–$25 each. Salt and pepper shaker sets are worth $25 for gold crest and $35 for blue and yellow. A large amount of CP Air china also is now seen for sale, as the airline changed its name recently; the value of these china pieces is $5–$10 each; salt and pepper shaker sets are valued at $25.

In 1986, Western Airlines began using a new china pattern in honor of its sixtieth anniversary. This very attractive china has a blue-and-gold shield with a logo, an Indian head, and the year 1926. This pattern had a short life-span, as Western merged into Delta in late 1986. Much of this china was sold to airline employees, but some has shown up on the secondary markets in recent months. Although plentiful now, this pattern is attractive and its short period of usage will probably make it valuable in years to come.

Plastic or Bakelite items, even though possibly old, have a minimal value, usually $1–$2. Pieces with a nice, older logo on the side appear on the market in the $5 range.

China pieces from sets in current use by domestic carriers and those in use by sizable foreign carriers (such as British Airways, Air Canada, Lufthansa) carry a value of about $5 each. Older pieces are valued in the $25 range, as are any items from very small foreign carriers. As a general rule, pieces which are top-marked with an airline name and/or logo and which can be documented as being from the 1940s era are valued in the $50–$100 range. China from the Pan Am flying boat era is valued at $100–$150. The cup and saucer sets are small, and thus easily taken as "souvenirs." They appear to be the most commonly seen pieces of this pattern, so the larger pieces are more rare, and in this instance equally or more valuable. Documented prewar pieces of any kind are valued at $100 and up, with the American Airlines DC-3 pieces being perhaps the most valuable (in the $200 range). Bear in mind that china collectors favor pieces such as cup and saucer sets and dinner plates, and as such, these pieces will carry a premium of up to 50 percent over the prices of other pieces of the same pattern.

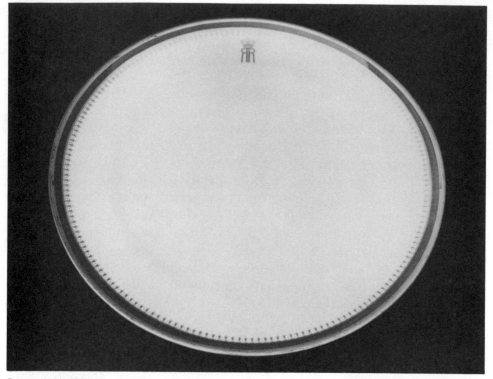

Regent Air 10½" dinner plate; unusually large for an airline plate, but then Regent was an unusual airline. Made by Spode; blue and gold pattern. **$100**

Pan Am demitasse cup and saucer from service known as "The President"; Noritake china. **$35** set

United cup and saucer set from the airline's Red Carpet Room airport clubroom; Syracuse china, 1960s. **$15** set

United cup and saucer set with silver rim and logo on a white china. Although from a large airline, this pattern apparently was used only for a short time, and pieces seldom turn up. Bears no manufacturer's name. **$35** set

Russia's Aeroflot china carries an attractive blue stripe, gold rings, and the Aeroflot logo. A 3" vegetable dish is pictured. **$10**

Believed to be an early Western Airlines china pattern, which bears a 1942 date code. Dark red design on light brown Syracuse china. **$75**

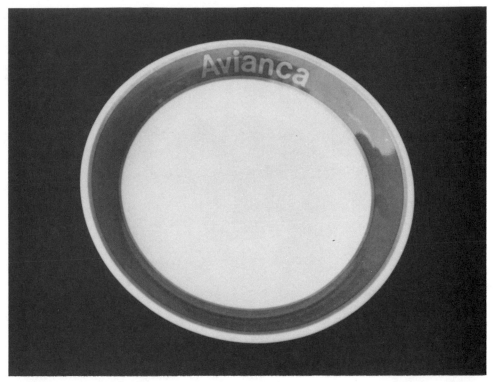

Beautiful burgundy and gold markings on this dish from Avianca, Colombia's national airline; Noritake china. **$25**

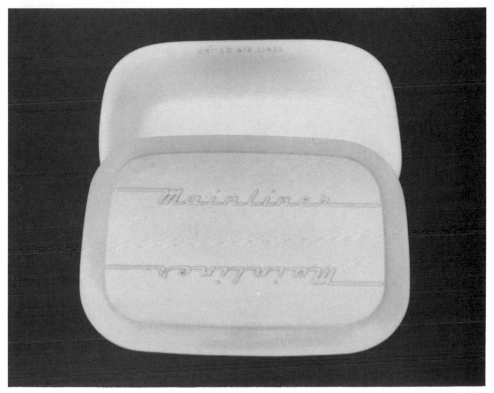

United DC-3 era china. Dish has light blue sides and United name; Hall china. A plastic light blue lid kept the entree hot; lid carried the Mainliner name (the DC-3 designation). **$25** set

TWA Royal Ambassador cup and saucer set. Has red stripe and gold RA crest, TWA name on bottom of each piece; Rosenthal china. **$15** set

United "swirl" pattern cup and saucer with gold rim and logo on white china. Since the china is very delicate, unbroken pieces without major wear on the gold trim are hard to find. **$35** set

Pakistan International Airlines cup and saucer set with gold trim on white china, made by Cloudland. **$35** set

TWA cup and saucer is similar to the Royal Ambassador style, but this has the red stripe split into four stripes and TWA instead of RA in the gold crest. Various manufacturers produced this china including Abco, Michaud, and Racket. **$10** set

Demitasse cup with black lettering and red and blue logo, and a casserole with blue logo, from Texas International, the small regional carrier owned by Frank Lorenzo prior to his takeover of Continental and Eastern Airlines. **$35** each

This small and delicate Pan Am cup and saucer is from the flying boat era; Homer Laughlin china. **$125** set

Pan Am china made by Johann Haviland in honor of the 25th anniversary of the first jet service to Europe. The black and white china bears the anniversary marking on the bottom. **$20** set

Small, single egg cup from CAAC, mainland China's national airline. **$10**

Continental sake cups are very small, only 1½" high by 1½" wide; both are Noritake china. A cup with Continental's new logo is shown at left, **$10;** a cup bearing the old logo is at right. **$20**

Piedmont Airline coffee cup with bluebird logo on side. Piedmont merged into USAir in 1989. Hall china. **$10**

A small and short-lived airline, McClain had its logo and name only on the coffee cup. Pieces have attractive gold and blue trim; Rego china. **$20** set

An attractive china in a burgundy, tan, and gold pattern, used by Northwest Airlines on international flights. The china is called Regal Imperial; made by Royal Doulton. **$25** set

Northeast Airlines "yellowbird" coffee mug; Hall china. **$20**

Western Airlines 2" tall individual creamer. Small creamers were occasionally found in railroad china, but this is the only airline example of which the author is aware. Abco china. **$5**

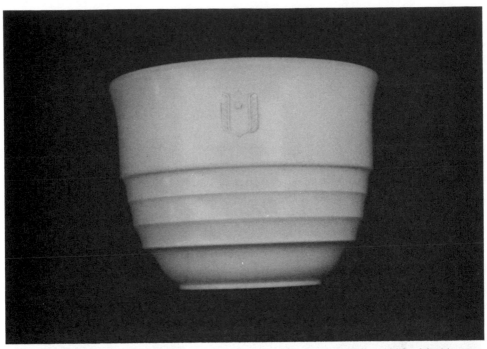

An early plastic piece, light blue, used by United beginning in the 1930s. Marking on side is identical to handle of silver flatware used during same period. **$5**

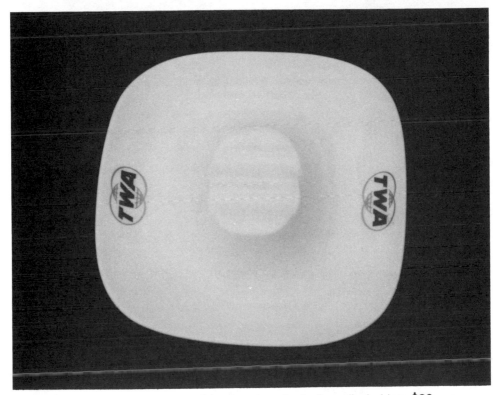

Not a cheap advertising ashtray, this piece is actually Rosenthal china. **$20**

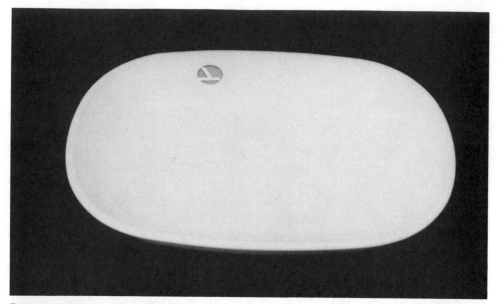

Eastern Airlines casserole dish with blue logo. Very few Eastern pieces have a top-logo identification. Corning Ware. **$12**

Australian Airlines dish with flying kangaroo logo in gold; Wedgwood china. **$20**

Five fine-quality salt and pepper shakers. Left to right: Emirates Air, Air Mauritius, British Airways, Virgin Atlantic, and the unique British Airways Concorde pattern. The two British Airways examples and the Emirates piece are Royal Doulton china; the other two are Wedgwood. **$25–$35** per set

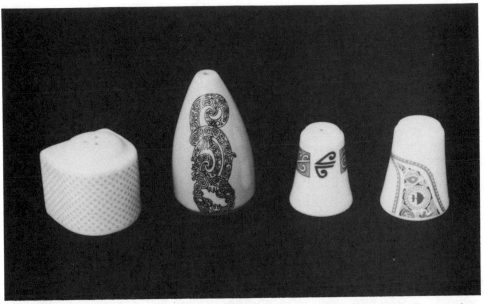

Some unusual-shaped salt and pepper shakers. Left to right: one from Lufthansa, two from Air New Zealand, and one from Malaysian Air System. The two on the left are Hutschenreuther and Crown Lynn china, respectively; the two on the right are Noritake. **$25–$35** set

American Airlines dark blue china with platinum stripe, used in international first class service. Only the dinner plate in this pattern has the eagle logo on top. A large number of pieces of this china are on the secondary market at present; these pieces are thought to be manufacturers' rejects. The various makers are Jackson, Sterling, Syracuse, and probably others. Plate, **$15;** other pieces, **$3–$5.**

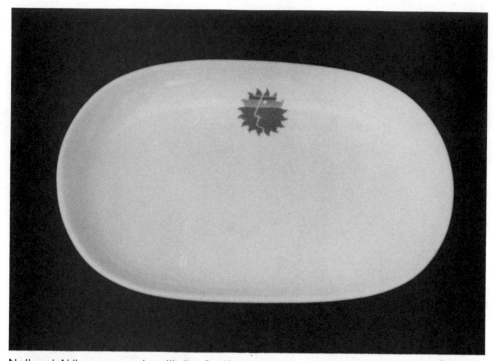

National Airlines casserole with the SunKing logo in brown; Sterling China Co. **$25**

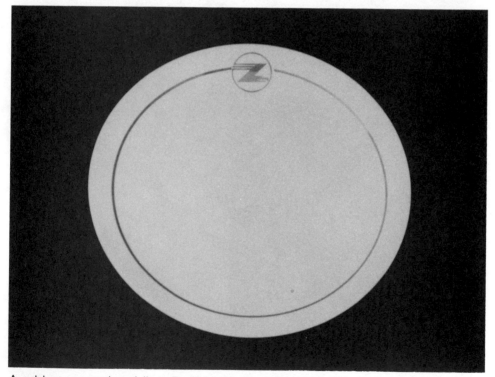

A seldom-encountered line, Zambia Airways, uses this attractive green and yellow pattern; Wedgwood china. **$20**

An old, rare Braniff pattern with the shield logo in gold; Real china (Brazil). **$20**

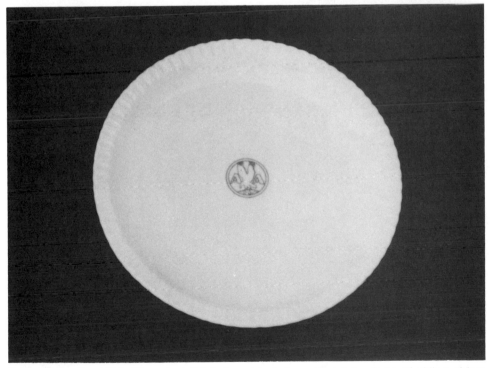

Dating from the 1935–37 period, this is the oldest documentable piece of airline china which the author has found. American logo in light blue gives clues to age; the eagle is facing left, and the legs of the letters are of unequal thickness. Syracuse "Shelledge" china. **$200**

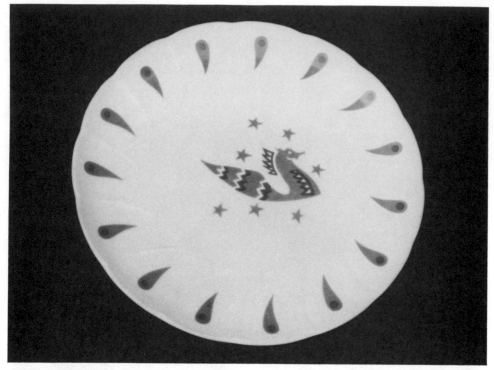

Air France blue and yellow china pattern, prominently featuring the seahorse logo; Limoges china **$25**

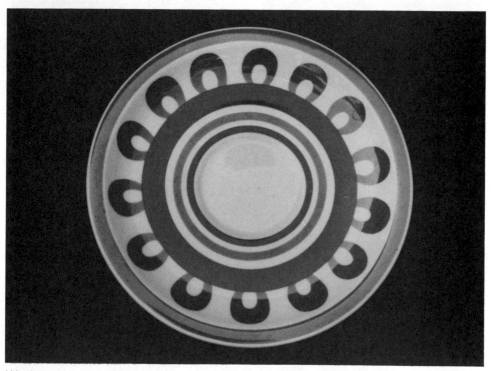

Western Airlines used this gaudy red and blue china pattern for a time. Although not as elegant as most airline china, china in this pattern is rare and valuable. The only clue to airline origin is the small "WAL" initials on back. Block china (Portugal). **$25**

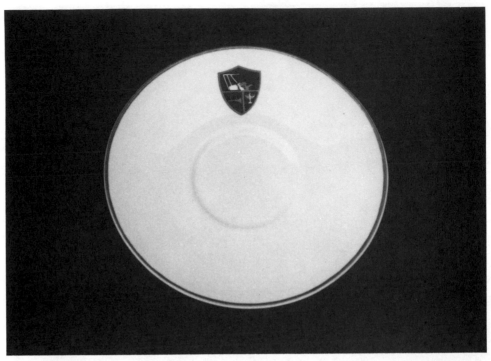

Older Western Airlines pattern featured a black shield with "Wallybird" parrot mascot, a trumpet, and champagne glass, all in gold. Mayer china. **$15**

Brazil's Varig Airlines uses this silver and gray pattern. Noritake china. **$15**

Pan Am plate from the mid-1940s with dark blue markings. This is a heavy-weight, industrial-grade china seldom found in airline service. Walker china. **$100**

An early TWA dish in clear glass. Six of these fit into a rack inside a stainless steel insulated canister that kept meals hot. Used during the 1930s and 1940s in planes which had no galleys or facilities for heating food (see page 80). **$25**

The famous "Airlite" china made for American by Scyracuse just after the war. Only three pieces were in the set. All three pieces had the pattern, makers, and airline names on the bottom; the salad dish had no stars or logo. Dish, **$30;** cup, **$50;** plate, **$100.**

Delta's red and blue widget logo china is the most common of all airline china. Various domestic and foreign manufacturers. **$2–$3** per piece

Lan Chile demitasse set in dark blue and gold; Florencia china (Chile). **$30** set

Trans Brasil green and white demitasse set with an unusual square-shaped saucer. Real china (Brazil). **$25** set

Attractive and unique British Airways pattern used only on the Concorde. The pattern depicts the shape of the Concorde plane in yellow and is repeated on a blue background; Royal Doulton china. **$30** set

Kuwait Airways china pattern trimmed in two shades of blue and pink. Hutschenreuther china. **$35** set

JAT, Yugoslavia's national airline, used this attractive wine-red pattern. Unusual feature is the diamond logo (at left on saucer) of the manufacturer Titov Veles (Yugoslavia). Communist bloc countries have few planes with business or first class compartments, and the dinnerware is difficult to obtain. **$40**

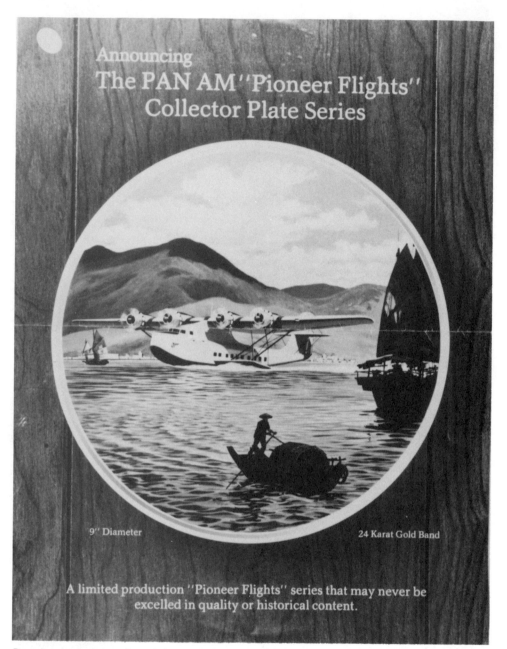

Announcing
The PAN AM "Pioneer Flights"
Collector Plate Series

9" Diameter

24 Karat Gold Band

A limited production "Pioneer Flights" series that may never be
excelled in quality or historical content.

Pan Am issued a series of six collector plates depicting historic aircraft (three of them flying boats); from color paintings by Bauscher Weiden. The plates are very attractive but are still available on the market at about the same price as when issued 15 years ago. **$25–$30** each

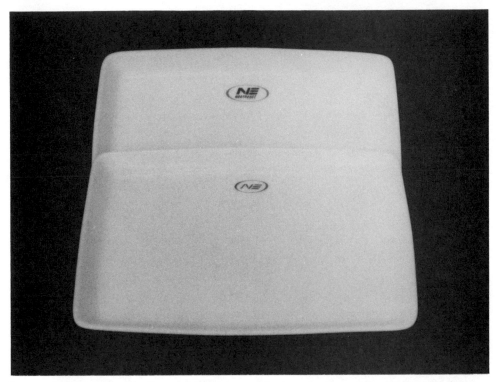

Two variations of the Northeast Airlines logo prior to adoption of the "yellowbird" logo. Both are Noritake china. **$40** each

4 Crystal and Glassware

Collecting glassware is almost as popular as collecting china. Glassware is found more often in flea market settings and can be purchased in a wide variety of sizes, shapes, and styles from many airlines.

Unfortunately, it is not possible to date glassware as precisely as china, since glassware usually does not have the maker's name and date code as does most china. The airline logo must be used as the chief clue to age. In some cases, airlines such as Eastern used Rosenthal crystal ware (which does bear their manufacturing marking) for service during a specific era, so an approximate dating can be obtained. British Airways recently began using Royal Doulton–marked glassware in its first class and Concorde service.

Glassware can be found from nearly every airline of any size, because it is an inexpensive item to use for promotional purposes, even if the airline doesn't actually use it for in-flight beverage service.

Generally, the most desired glassware are those pieces which were actually used in beverage service on board flights. Another category is souvenir glasses, usually sold by the airlines from a gift catalog. Eastern issued a number of special glasses to commemorate its Silver Falcon, Golden Falcon, and Constellation aircraft types. On the back of some, in script, was ''Compliments of Eddie Rickenbacker''—Eastern's long-time war-hero president. These glasses are quite popular and valuable. The third category includes glasses issued by some airlines as promotional items and distributed primarily to travel agents and employees.

It is somewhat difficult to make general rules about the value of glassware. The usual rules about the size of the airline, and the age of glass, etc., apply, but there are significant exceptions. Crystal pieces are always desirable; if a piece is lacking a manufacturer's mark, you can usually identify crystal by the ''ring'' sound if you flip a finger against the glass rim.

Two of today's major airlines, Delta and TWA, currently do not use marked glassware. Their marked glassware from in-flight service in years past is more valuable than would otherwise be the case for glassware from large-size carriers. Over the years, American, Continental, Eastern, Northwest, Pan Am, and United have used many styles of glasses with various logos. Something in the range of 15 to 30 different types of glassware exist for each of these airlines.

Pan Am also issued a number of souvenir glasses, as well as a number of special glasses for single-charter flights. For example, a Shriners trip to Greece and a Georgia Tech University alumni jaunt to Rome each rated cocktail glasses with the organization's logo (as well as Pan Am's), plus the date and destination.

Glassware is more common than china on today's collectible's market, as the pieces are smaller and more often carried off flights as souvenirs; in addition, a large number of glasses have been given or sold as promo items. As a general rule, current glasses from domestic and large foreign carriers will carry a value between $2 and $5; sellers usually charge double that amount for items from smaller, foreign airlines. The Eastern Rickenbacker glasses bring $15–$20 each, because they are one of the most valuable examples of glasses not used for regular in-flight service. The most valuable items used in in-flight service would probably be the elegant leaded crystal pieces made in Portugal for Regent Air by Atlantis. These reportedly cost the airline $30–$65 each, depending on size; their value as a collectible would be the same amount.

Southern Airways issued a series of souvenir shot glasses during each of its 30 years of existence. The first glass, issued in 1949, now brings a price of $500–$600, with the latter 29 ranging from $35 down to $5 each.

Piece typical of the glassware used by Piedmont in its first class service. **$10**

SAHSA is the Honduras national carrier. Logo design indicates the line was probably organized by and controlled by Pan Am at one time. **$25**

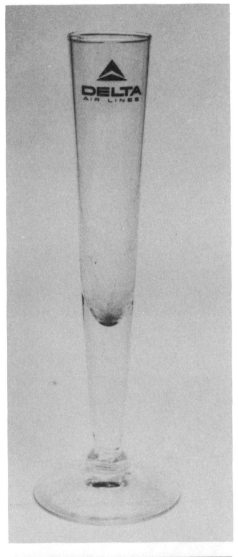

Unusual vase with a gold Delta logo. **$20**

Tall Ozark wine glass, probably a gift catalog item **$8**

A very heavy and exquisite Regent Air leaded-crystal cocktail glass, made by Atlantis (Portugal). **$35**

Eastern Airlines glass, believed to be from the 1930s. **$25**

Current American Airlines wine glass showing the most modern version of the over-50-year-old eagle logo. **$4**

Two older Eastern logo styles. Version at left is from the 1950s. The version at right was used for only a short time in the 1960s; after that a modernized version of the falcon was adopted. **$20** each

Two examples of Pan Am glasses created solely for a single charter flight. **$10** each

Two pieces of Eastern crystal ware made by Rosenthal. The delicate nature of the glass is evident from the photo. **$20** each

A crystal brandy glass with an unusual location for the Eastern logo. Made by Schott Zweisel, Germany. **$16**

TWA crystal wine glass used in the airline's original Royal Ambassador service. **$20**

Current style of Eastern glassware; very common. **$2**

United wine glass with its older shield logo. Although many styles of glassware had this logo, all are in demand. **$5–$10**

Pretty glass from Royal Air Maroc (Morocco). **$10**

Unusual inaugural-flight glass with logos of two different airlines. **$10**

This glass with gold designs was issued to mark Pan Am's Boeing 727 inaugural flight to Central and South America. **$20**

SunKing logo is seen on a variety of glasses from National Airlines. **$5–$10**

Roly-poly glass from Russia's Aeroflot; gold logo. **$20**

Allegheny roly-poly glass with the airline's name and logo in red and blue. **$10**

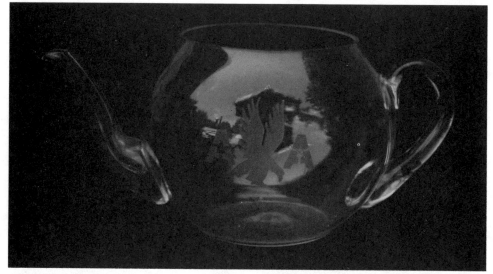

Unusual glass teapot from American; $3\frac{1}{2}''$ tall. **$50**

Individual coffee server with blue glass American Airlines logo. **$35**

TWA souvenir glasses; the one at right has a plastic overlay. **$7** each

Small United wine carafe with gold logo and scrollwork. **$15**

Three of Eastern's glasses, each commemorating new aircraft types. **$15–$20** each

Three Continental roly-poly glasses with different versions of the airline's Thunderbird logo. All are marked in gold. **$15** each

American roly-poly glass marked in silver. **$10**

Mexicana's 50th anniversary was commemorated with this gold and black marked glass. **$15**

One of a set of four souvenir glasses issued by Mohawk; each depicts a different type of aircraft Mohawk operated. **$15** each

TWA issued several different sets of souvenir glasses, naming the various countries to which it flies. **$5** each

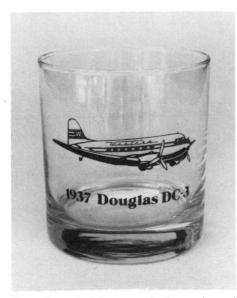

One of a set of six souvenir glasses issued by Western Airlines; each shows a type of aircraft the airline operated. These came out just before Delta took over Western and are hard to find. **$10** each

Smoked-glass piece marking Delta's 50th anniversary. **$10**

Northwest and Eastern salt and pepper shakers. **$8** set

Unusual wine glass from Avensa, a Venezuelan carrier. Base and stem are deep blue. **$10**

Glass with heavy base; British Caledonian. **$15**

Cocktail glass from TACA, the airline of El Salvador. **$10**

British Airways glass now used in first class and Concorde service, made by Royal Doulton. **$10**

Very finely cut glass crystal ware from Aeronaves de Mexico, the former name of Aeromexico. **$25**

Set of six glasses; believed to be non-airline issue but commonly sold as airline collectibles. The colorful markings are attractive and have proved durable. Each glass has "France" in small letters on the back. **$2–$3** each

Five of the famous Southern Airways anniversary shot glasses. Shown are glasses from the 10th, 15th, 20th, 25th, and 30th years. The 30th-year glass was the last one made. Price range is **$35** to **$5,** from left to right. (From the John R. Joiner collection.)

Souvenir shot glass with Southern, Republic, and Northwest logos. Only 300 were made, for a retired employee gathering; very hard to find. **$25** (From the John R. Joiner collection.)

The 3rd, 4th, 5th, and 6th-year Southern Airways shot glasses (1952–55), **$35** each. (From the John R. Joiner collection.)

5 Miscellaneous Dining-Service Items

Serving Pieces

Probably the most attractive airline dining service items, but the hardest to find, are the serving pieces used by flight attendants. These pieces consist primarily of trays, coffee pots, cream pitchers, sugar bowls, and sauce boats. Again, these items are used mainly in first class service, but even so, some airlines have gone from silver plate to stainless items in recent years.

For the silver-plate items, the collector should be discriminating when evaluating the condition of the items. Pieces which have dents and/or surface scratches and nicks are worth far less than comparable pieces that shine like a mirror. A small number of "war scars" is acceptable, but pieces showing long years of hard use should be avoided, unless they can be acquired for a very low price. Damaged pieces can be repaired and replated, but the replating often fills in and diminishes the crispness of the markings.

The most commonly found item, used mainly in the coach sections, is the traditional round stainless coffee urn, which is made to be clamped into the coffee maker in the galley. These are usually marked with the airline name and logo on the collar strap to which the handle is attached. In recent years, newer urns have the airline initials frosted on the side of the pot, and some examples seen recently do not have any marking at all. They are worth approximately $5–$10.

Silver-plate trays with a nice logo on the top are worth $50–$100; bottom-marked examples are worth half that amount.

Nice silver-plate coffee pitchers with a name or logo prominently marked on the side would be worth $75–$200 depending on age and condition. Pitchers with the airline's name or logo marked on the bottom would go for a price of $25–$75.

Cream pitchers, sugar bowls, and sauce boats have a value similar to the value of coffee pots, although slightly less, being smaller pieces. Side-marked examples are valued at $50–$150, and bottom-marked pieces are found in the $15–$35 range.

Stainless steel serving pieces have been used more recently, and usually are marked only on the bottom. They are worth much less than their silver-plate counterparts. Stainless trays are worth $10–$25; pitchers of all sizes, sugar bowls, and sauce boats are usually priced at $15–$35.

Flatware

Of all the items used on board a flight, flatware seems to be the most commonly-found collectible. Knives, forks, and spoons just seem to "wander" off planes. Over the years, airlines have dumped probably millions of pieces onto the secondary markets whenever they changed their pattern or logo or underwent a merger. Airline flatware is commonly seen at most flea markets and thrift stores. This availability makes it a popular and generally inexpensive collectible. An attractive and diverse collection can be had for a small cost.

On most airlines, older flatware was silver plate, but in the 1960s most of it was replaced with stainless. Today most airlines still use silver plate in first class and stainless for some meals in coach. Marked silver-plate flatware items can be found for some of the older airlines, even those airlines which didn't use marked china or glassware. Prior to the 1960s, plastic had not been developed yet to the point of being strong enough for flatware.

The most famous of all flatware is the Flagship pattern used by American Airlines in the 1930s–40s. The handle on each of these pieces is in the shape of a DC-3 fuselage nose. In those days, airlines had nicknames for their planes; American called theirs Flagships, perhaps in part because the American logo at that time was the AA and eagle logo in a pennant-shaped flag. Flagship flatware pieces in good condition bring $25 each; with moderate wear they are worth $20. An interesting variation on the knives (and possibly of the other two pieces) was a plain handle with the plane nose stamped in it. These are worth $20. A pickle fork in the Flagship pattern has been found recently; this rare companion piece is worth $35.

Most other silver-plate flatware is worth $2–$5, but there are exceptions. Pieces from smaller airlines that merged or went out of business years ago are worth $10–$25; examples are Capital, Penn Central, Chicago & Southern, Northeast, and Mid Continent. A similar value range applies to pieces with an older logo or marking from the prewar era from one of the larger lines, such as Braniff, Delta, Eastern, TWA, United, and Western.

Stainless flatware is almost without exception a low-ticket item; a value of 25¢ to 75¢ is common on most pieces. The law of supply and demand provides the guidelines to the value of pieces in this category. An airline with several hundred planes, each seating at least a hundred passengers, may serve several meals daily to each passenger, using three pieces of flatware for each passenger. There are always extra pieces on hand or being cleaned by the catering contractors at several dozen locations. Do a little multiplication and the number of pieces in existence easily swells to the hundreds of thousands. Even the most exotic stainless pieces, from a faraway or obscure foreign carrier, are worth only $2–$4.

Salt and Pepper Shakers

An interesting collectible, salt and pepper shakers have been produced in many sizes, shapes, and materials over the years for various airlines. As those who frequently fly these days know, small paper packets for salt and pepper are used in coach on most airlines, while in first class most domestic carriers use shakers made of glass with a metal cap. Most of the glass examples used today are generic-looking (no name or logo), but surprisingly, two of the most tightfisted carriers, Eastern and Northwest, use marked glass shakers. Marked glass examples are worth $2–$4 each.

In the 1930s, American Airlines used nickel-silver salt and pepper shakers made by International Silver Co. They had a sliding lid, with the airline name and "Salt" or "Pepper" on the top. The story is told that American began using these in the hope that people would take them as souvenirs, rather than the flagship flatware, which had been disappearing from meal trays at an alarming rate. The pepper shakers are worth $15, and the salt shakers are worth $25. Many of the salt shakers became corroded over the years, making them more scarce and thus more valuable.

Other early examples of salt and pepper shakers are made of plastic (Bakelite), most notably on TWA and United; these have the airline logo decal on them and are worth $5–$10 each, depending on the condition of the airline decal. Another early version is a heavy paper cylinder, about the same diameter as a large pencil, with a metal base and paper lid, used by Northwest. If nicely marked with a colorful logo, these shakers are worth $5 each.

The real crown jewels of salt and peppers are china pieces used on some of the foreign carriers, made by such manufacturers as Wedgwood and Royal Doulton. Some of the carriers using these items include Air Maritius, Air New Zealand, British Airways, Emirates Air Services, Laker Airways, Lufthansa, Malaysian Airlines System, Royal Jordanian, and Virgin Atlantic. Royal Jordanian has a very elegant set of shakers—a small china base with the Royal Jordanian logo houses the shakers. Most china shakers are worth $15–$35 per set.

Swizzle Sticks

A widely collected, attractive, and inexpensive item is the drink stirrer, commonly known as a swizzle. Most swizzle sticks are made of plastic (although a few metal and glass examples exist). Nearly every airline of any size has used swizzles over the years and they have come in all sizes and shapes. TWA used a red propeller-shaped model for several years in the 1970s. Braniff had a surfboard swizzle, American had a tennis racket-shaped swizzle, Eastern had a golf club variety, and the list goes on.

Several designs with a plane on the end appeared when the first jets were used. TWA used a set of swizzle sticks with a different country on each, and each one of those came in several different colors. New sticks are coming out all the time, making this segment of the airline collectibles hobby very active. Most swizzles are worth 25¢–50¢, but older examples with an old logo are worth up to $5.

Menus

Menus have been used over the years by the airlines, but they were most common during the postwar years. Originally used for all classes of service, today they are used only in first class on most flights. Some of the foreign carriers have issued very fancy and elaborate menus. In the past few years, Pan Am has used a set of 13 different menus featuring color paintings of vintage Pan Am planes. A miniature version of the same menu is used in Pan Am's business class section. Most are worth $2–$5, with very nice attractive older menus valued at $5–$10.

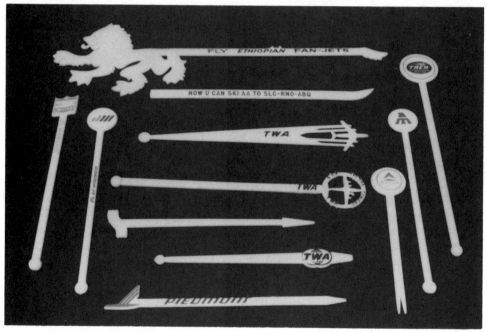

A variety of logo-marked swizzle sticks. The Ethiopian one at the top is nearly 10" long— their drinks must be something! Ethiopian **$3;** others **50¢–$2.**

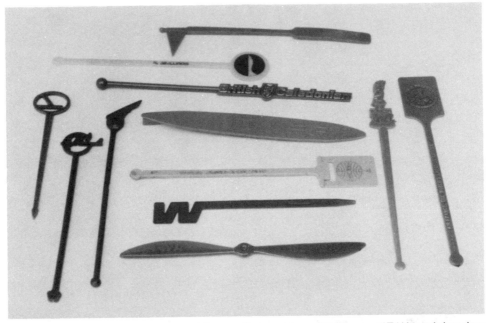

Swizzles of various colors, sizes, and shapes. Second from right is one of TWA's set showing 15 different countries. Old Pan Am winged-globe design, third from left, **$3;** all others, **50¢–$1.**

Three napkins: Air Atlanta 1985; Delta 1958; and American 1940. Value **$5, $10,** and **$25,** respectively.

Three TWA silver-plate flatware patterns from the 1950–70 era. Top, **$5**; middle, **$2**; bottom, **$3.**

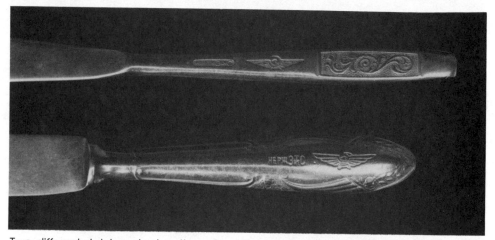

Two different stainless steel patterns from Russia's Aeroflot. Although these pieces are not very old they are difficult to find. **$3–$5**

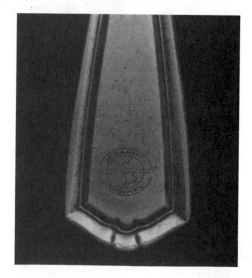

Braniff pattern from the 1940s, shortly after Braniff adopted "International" as a nickname. **$10**

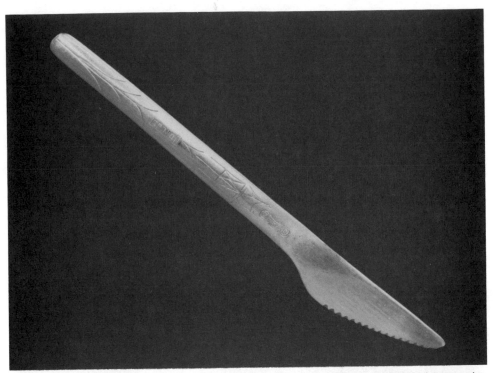

Fancy stainless steel knife from Garuda Indonesian Airways. Reverse side is just as ornate, but in a different pattern. **$2**

Early Chicago & Southern silver-plate spoon, probably from the 1940s. **$10**

Ornate pattern on stainless steel spoon; pattern used by Ecuatoriana, the flag carrier of Ecuador. Note E logo on shank. **$3**

Pacific Northern silver-plate spoon; 1950s. **$10**

Early TWA fork showing the logo used from the early 1930s until World War II. Silver plate; very rare. **$35**

Iraqi Airways fork, probably 1970s; hard to find. **$4**

Early United silver-plate pattern, probably from the 1930s. On the back are three words: "United Air Lines." **$7**

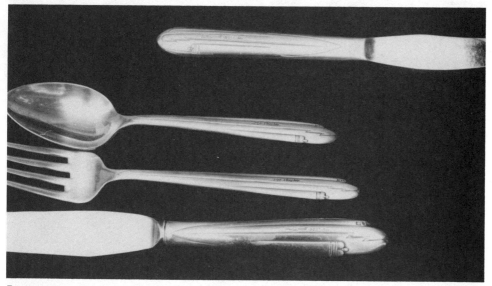

Famous American Airlines Flagship silver-plate pattern from the 1930s. Variation at top has DC3 nose stamped on a flat solid knife handle; **$20–$25** each. Pickle fork also known to exist, **$35.**

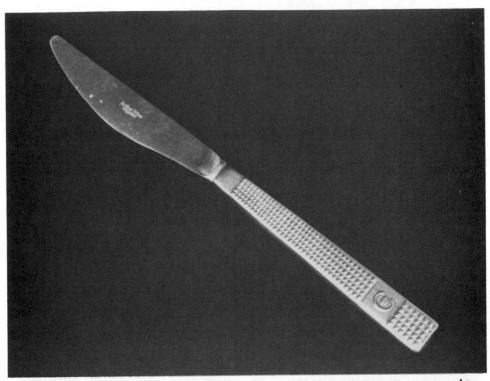

Recent British Airways silver-plate pattern used for the airline's Concorde service. **$3**

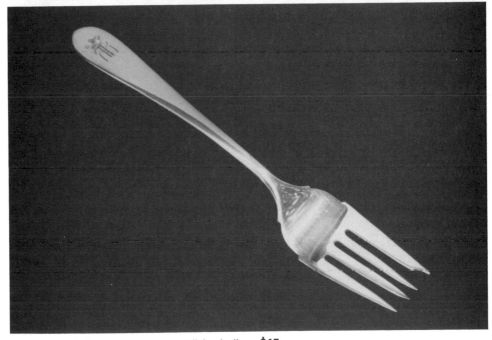

Regent Air fork; very heavy, possibly sterling. **$15**

Liquor miniatures, formerly packaged for different airlines. Empties, **$1–$3;** full bottles, **$5–$10.**

Part of the set of 13 menus used by Pan Am; each shows a color painting of an historic aircraft. **$15–$20** per set

Two TWA menus from the 1960s. **$4** each

TWA Bakelite meal tray from the late 1940s. **$20**

Large United serving tray by International Silver Co, made during the 1960s. **$75**

TWA coffee serving set by International Silver Co.; 1960s. For nice condition (as pictured): tray, **$75;** coffee pot, **$75;** cream pitcher, **$50.** Add 50 percent if mint; deduct 50 percent if heavily used.

United sugar and creamer by Reed & Barton, 1960s vintage. **$25–$35** each

Some of the last silver-plate items used by TWA, made by Oneida during the 1970s. Both coffee and cream pitcher are common. **$15–$20** each

Serving set from Eastern Airlines' Famous Restaurants Flights during the 1960s; Reed & Barton silver plate. Although marked with Eastern's logo on the bottom, these pieces are among the most elegant ever seen in airline service. Large pitchers, **$100** each; small pitcher, **$75;** sugar bowl, **$50.**

American's little thimble-sized nickel silver salt and peppers from the 1930s. Pepper, **$15;** salt, **$25.**

Three American pieces from the 1950s. Tea pitcher, **$75;** butter cup, **$50;** tray, **$50.**
Tray is believed to be a gift given to passengers on certain flights.

Large Pan Am coffee pitcher from the 1940s made by International Silver Co. **$200**

American silver-plate napkin rings and small plate. **$25** each

TWA hot food canister from the 1940s. Contains a rack with six glass dishes. Canister is insulated and was used on planes which had no galleys or food heating facilities. A relic of the early days of commercial flight food service. **$250**

6 Crew and Ground Personnel Items

Wings and Badges

Wings and badges are popular collectible items, and a few examples find their way into just about every sizable collection of aviation items.

Wings and badges have been used since the first days of aviation, and many varieties exist from the larger airlines. There are distinctive designs for captains (pilots), first officers (copilots), and second officers (flight engineers). Some are gold, some are brass, some are sterling, and some are nickel. At one time stewardesses wore small caps which had wings on them, and lapel wings are worn today on the uniform coats of the flight attendants and of the flight deck crew.

As a general rule, even wings and badges in current use are worth a minimum of $25, because that is approximately the cost to the airlines today. Older examples are valued by collectors at up to several hundred dollars for rare pieces. To estimate value, the age of the piece and the size of the airline must be taken into account. Other things being equal, wings generally are worth more than badges.

Uniforms

Uniforms are not a widely collected item, due to the relatively large amount of space needed to display them. But a nice coat and cap with the buttons, badges, and wings can make an attractive display item. Caps are worth $5–$10, and uniforms are worth $10–$50. These prices are for the caps and uniforms (with buttons) only. If wings and/or badges are included, their value must be added. Neckties featuring the airline logo, usually as a part of the design, are often worn by flight attendants and are seen for sale in the $5–$10 range.

Service Pins

Service pins are small lapel pins given by the airlines to employees in recognition of years of service, usually at five-year intervals. They feature the airline's logo and the number of years served. Some also include precious stones. Service pins are not a common item, making them very desirable and collectible. Depending on the size of the airline, attractiveness of design, and whether stones are present, the value range is $10–$100.

Patches

Large embroidered patches with the airline name or logo once worn by ramp and service personnel are worth $5–$10.

Pilot's cap from Aeroflot. **$100**

Two National Airlines caps, showing the old logo of a flag (left) and the new SunKing design (right). Left, **$75;** right, **$50.**

Cap badge and wings from Cascade Airways, a regional carrier in the Pacific Northwest region of the United States. **$50** each

Wings from Wien Air Alaska. **$85**

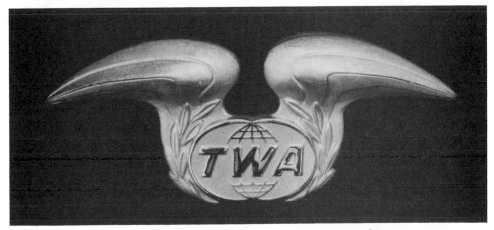

TWA cap badge, reportedly used by certain ground personnel. **$35**

Stewardess wings from Britt Airways, a regional carrier in the midwest United States. **$35**

Wings from Aeromexico (top) and wings from when the airline went by the name Aeronaves de Mexico (bottom). **$35** each

Ozark wings from the 1970s. **$45**

Frontier wings, with wine-red porcelain background. This was Frontier's last wing design. **$50**

TWA cap badge; same style is in current use, but made from lightweight metal. **$35**

Kansas City Southern Skyways badge. This short-lived cargo operation was a subsidiary of the KCS Railroad, which used the same logo; **$150.** (From the John R. Joiner collection.)

Northeast Airlines wings showing Pilgrim logo, **$150.** (From the John R. Joiner collection.)

First TWA pilot wings issued after the Trans World Airlines name was adopted (top), **$125.** Early stewardess wings worn on cap (1936), **$100.** (From the John R. Joiner collection.)

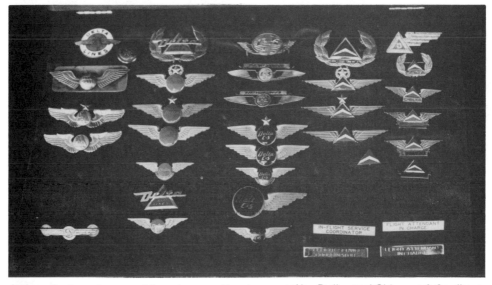

A nice display of many of the wings and badges used by Delta and Chicago & Southern over the years. For a few years after Delta absorbed C&S, the airline operated under the name Delta C&S, as shown on some of the items in the center row. Value of items pictured ranges from **$25** to **$200.** (From the John R. Joiner collection.)

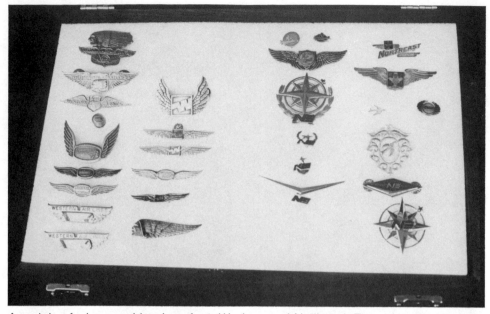

A variety of wings and badges from Western and Northeast. The value range of the items pictured is **$50** to **$200.** (From the John R. Joiner collection.)

Early badge and wings from T&WA, the airline which resulted from the merger of Transcontinental Air Transport and Western Air Express. Many years later, the same TWA initials would come in handy when the name was changed to Trans World Airlines; **$250** each (From the John R. Joiner collection.)

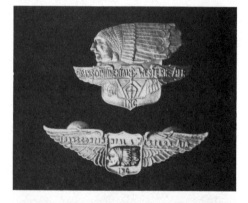

The five cap badges pictured are those used by Southern Airways during its 30-year history. Camp Wolters, Texas, was a military base used for pilot training. Price range for items shown, **$75–$125.** (From the John R. Joiner collection.)

American Airlines sterling silver wings from the 1930s. **$85**

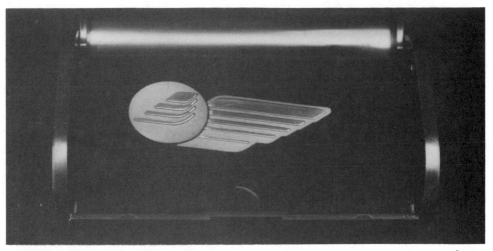

Flight attendant wing from Air Atlanta, the small and short-lived Georgia carrier. **$30**

TWA service pin with red enamel background from the 1940s. **$30**

7 Timetables and Brochures

Timetable values are mainly based on age. The size of the airline also is important. Generally, timetables from 1970 to the present are of minimal value (25¢–$1) because so many have been printed and distributed during this period.

Timetables of the 1950–69 era are somewhat more desirable, as they highlight the pinnacle of the propeller craft and the early jet eras. The value of these timetables is $2–$5.

The 1940s era represents the period of maturity for the major lines. Timetables for the war years are somewhat scarce and valued at $10–$20.

A lot happened to the airline industry in the 1930s; many of today's large carriers began operations in that decade. However, there was a turbulent period when the government canceled the all-important airmail contracts.

The Postmaster General had called a conference of airline officials to discuss airmail matters. But later, all airlines which took part in the conference were disqualified from further airmail contract bidding. The affected airlines easily conquered that hurdle by simply renaming their companies. Thus, in one short period, American Airways became American Airlines, Eastern Air Transport became Eastern Airlines, and so on. Timetables with names predating this change (1934) are highly desirable, but actually all 1930s items are scarce. Many small carriers came and went with only scant notice during the early 1930s, and even a pocket-size timetable, typically used by the tiny guys in those days, is a good find; their value range is $15–$75.

There were very few scheduled airlines prior to 1930, and their route structures were usually tiny. Timetables from this period are extremely rare and are valued in the range of $40–$100.

Brochures promoting travel on a particular airline are not quite as desirable as timetables, although some issues also include time schedules. The primary purpose of the brochure was to entice travel to a city or resort area served by the airline who issued it. Therefore, the brochures do most of their promoting on the attractions of the locale, rather than on the airline itself. Their value to collectors ranges from $1–$10, depending on age.

Pan Am booklet from the 1950s. The booklet tried to entice passengers to visit countries on Pan Am's Central and South American routes. **$10**

Delta's 50th anniversary paperback booklet covering the airline's history. **$5**

Western Airlines 60th anniversary paperback booklet detailing the airline's 60 years of history. **$5**

United air map of the United States from 1961. **$5**

Three TWA timetables from the early 1930s. The Ford trimotors pictured were the latest word in air travel at that time. **$35–$40** each

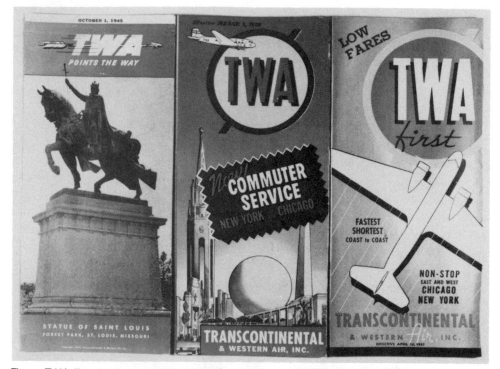

Three TWA timetables: 1945 (left), 1939 (center), and 1937 (right). The logo was simply TWA, although the initials of the actual corporation were T&WA. **$15–$20** each

Three interesting operations are represented by the timetables shown here. Varney was averaging five passengers a week when a fellow named Bob Six bought it and transformed it into today's Continental Airlines. C&S operated its X-shaped route with a handful of craft; Delta took it over in 1953. Century was owned by E. L. Cord (of Auburn-Cord-Dusenberg automobile fame) who later controlled American Airlines and merged Century into AA. **$35–$45** each

Three colorful Pan Am timetables from the 1930s, the era of the flying boat. **$25–$35** each

Early Eastern and Delta timetables, and a 1951 American Airlines edition promoting its hourly service between what were then the nation's two largest cities, Chicago and New York. American, **$15;** Delta and Eastern, **$20** each.

Alaska Star, formerly Star Airlines, later became Alaska Airlines. All-American started as a mail-only operation, and actually picked up mail using a cable and hook, without ever landing! Passenger service began later, and the name was changed to Allegheny. Pan Am used the Flying Clippers theme long after the real flying boats were gone. **$10–$15** each

Three small timetables from airlines of the 1930s that have been out of business for a long time. Boston-Maine Airways and Central Vermont Airways were operated by railroads of the same name. Despite all of the railroad mergers, these two railroads still exist today. **$35** each.

Early timetables (from the 1930s) of four of today's bigger airlines. United was still flying biplanes and Eastern hadn't yet changed its name to Eastern Airlines. **$40** each

Pan Am wasn't the only flying-boat operator, as these four timetables attest. Thompson is from 1929, the others from the 1930s. **$30** each

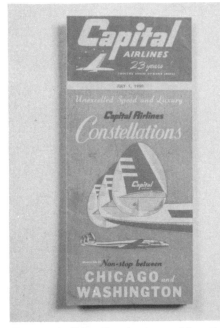

The most distinctive feature of the Constellation plane was its triple tail. The feature was promoted by Capital on this 1950 timetable. **$20**

Lufthansa timetable from 1934. The logo—the flying crane—has remained unchanged to this day. **$30**

Zeppelin timetable and brochure for the 1937 season, the last year Zeppelins flew. Graf Zeppelin's schedule was cancelled after the Hindenburg exploded. **$100** each

Colonial, Stout, and Wyoming were prominent carriers in the early 1930s. All three later became important parts of larger airlines. **$45** each

8 Advertising Items

The variety of advertising and promotional items used by the airlines is endless, with every gizmo, gadget, widget, and whatchamacallit imaginable currently available to collectors. A few items are more common than most, such as ashtrays made of glass, plastic, metal, etc.; these generally have a price range of $5–$10. Air India distributed statues of its Maharajah "mascot," ranging in size from a couple of inches to a couple of feet tall. Prices for these statues vary from $5 to $75. Royal Dutch Airlines (KLM) issued a set of small liquor bottles in the shape of Dutch houses. More than 50 different varieties of these bottles have been produced to date. With Delph-blue trim, these small houses are worth $15 and are a popular collectible among glass and china collectors, as well as among airline people.

Airline wall calendars are an attractive and popular collectible. Those from the 1930s and 1940s are sought most often as they generally feature plane pictures. Calendars of that era are valued at $25–$100. More recent examples usually depict scenes from the cities or countries served by the airline and are worth $5–$25.

Mugs for coffee and for beer have been a popular giveaway item for a number of years. Frequently these were given by the airline sales representatives to travel agents and major customers, or offered to the public through gift catalogs, or given to passengers. Most common of all are the squat china mugs with "Soup's on United" wording repeated around the sides; apparently these mugs were a passenger giveaway item. These mugs come with the lettering in various colors and are worth $1. Also common are the Lufthansa ceramic mugs of various sizes and designs, generally with the airline name and logo in blue on the side; these are worth $5. Other miscellaneous mugs are worth in the $5–$10 range.

Ceramic tiles have been issued by a few airlines as a collector's item. Most are 4" to 6" square, with abstract designs, usually incorporating the carrier's logo. Many different tiles were issued by KLM, and other airlines as well. Most are worth $5, but the unique United pair of tiles with planes on them are valued at $25 the pair.

Small slogan and advertising pins are a popular item from most airlines in recent years. Most are very small, the diameter of a dime or smaller.

A surprisingly large variety of pins have come from Aeroflot, the Russian national airline. Most of the pins are valued in the $1–$5 range.

In a class by itself is the category of airline advertising posters. Issued by airlines worldwide since the late 1920s, the early posters glamorized the concept of air travel and later depicted exotic destinations. Many of the early (i.e., prewar) examples are true works of art and are recognized and collected as such. Prices can range as high as $2,000 for rare early items, down to $5–$25 for most from the past 20 years or so.

Over the years, it has been traditional for airlines to obtain and distribute large models of their newest plane types. Such models generally have a wingspan and fuselage length ranging from 2' to 3', and they are often seen in travel agencies, as well as in the airlines' own ticket offices. Formerly made of metal, models have been made of plastic for approximately the past 15 years. The models are hard to find, and they are seldom seen for sale. The metal versions are the most valuable, ranging in price from $1,000–$2,500. The price range for the more recent plastic models is $300–$500.

Airlines issued a number of framed photographs primarily for display in their own offices, various ticket offices, and travel agencies. These generally were 16" × 20" (frame size) and usually had a color picture of a plane in flight. Nice, large framed pictures, with the airline name on the mat or frame, are hard to find, and are valued in the $50–$100 range.

Baggage stickers and labels have been distributed by the airlines from the very earliest days of operation. Usually quite colorful, these items are an extremely popular collectible. Several guidebooks have been issued, depicting the various examples and giving a value range for each. The stickers and labels go for as little as a dollar, but most are in the $5–$10 range, with some valued at up to $100.

Postcards are a popular collectible, and many hundreds of different examples exist. Most valuable are those actually issued by the airlines. These are worth 50¢ to $25, depending on age, rarity of airline, and type of plane depicted. Also, many postcards are available which were issued by various publishers.

Airlines also issued a variety of pictures, either in the form of 8" × 10" photographic prints or as lithographs, the latter sometimes being in color, suitable for framing. The 8" × 10" prints usually cost $1–$5, and lithographs, which are usually in a set, average $2–$3 each. United Airlines issued a set of about 10 brown-tone lithographs depicting various eras of flight history. United planes, naturally, are shown in most of the scenes. Surprising is the "United Airlines Photo" credit on the picture of the Wright Brothers' first flight! Value of this set is $5.

New York Rio & Buenos Aires was a short-lived flying-boat operator, lasting only six months during 1930. The airline had no mail contract and was forced to sell to Pan Am. Although slightly used, this colorful blotter is an extremely rare flying boat item. **$25**

Two tiles from KLM and one from TWA. **$5** each

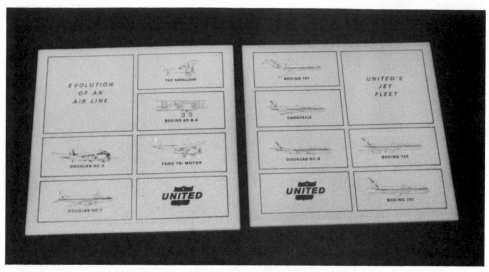

United distributed this attractive set of two 6" square glazed tiles. The frames and writing are in gold, while the aircraft are painted blue with red trim. They are felt-backed, with loops for hanging on the wall. **$25** set

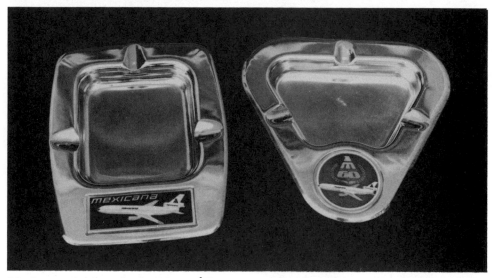

Mexicana stainless steel ashtrays. **$5**

Attractive small (4" round) red and white Capital Airlines ashtray. **$10**

102

Capital Airlines Christmas tree ornament, probably an employee giveaway. Fragile and unusual, it is unlikely that many of these survived, and no Capital collection is complete without one. **$20**

United issued this framed color photograph of a DC-6. Frame size is 19" × 22". **$65**

Certificates such as these were issued by a number of airlines during the era when ocean-crossing flights were a novelty. **$10**

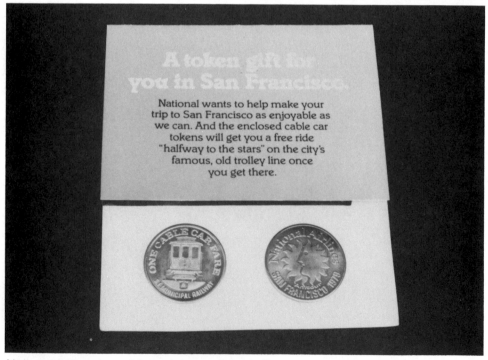

National Airlines issued these tokens, glued to the card, in 1979. The tokens were identical; each side is shown on the illustration. Card and tokens, **$5.**

One of a series of color lithographs, approximately 8″ × 10″, issued by Aeromexico to depict its historical craft. **$5**

Several varieties of ceramic, plastic, and metal ashtrays are illustrated here. Price range of items shown is **$5–$25.** (From the Shirley and Larry Ibsen collection.)

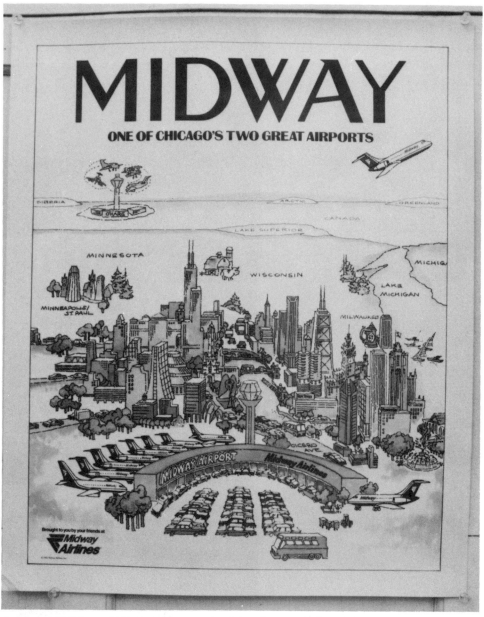

A comical Midway Airlines poster emphasizing the proximity of Midway Airport to downtown Chicago. The world's busiest airport, O'Hare, is shown in the upper left, seemingly in the middle of nowhere. **$5**

Large and colorful poster illustrates the lavish service accorded to international first and business class passengers on Northwest Orient. The poster shows off the Regal Imperial china. **$8**

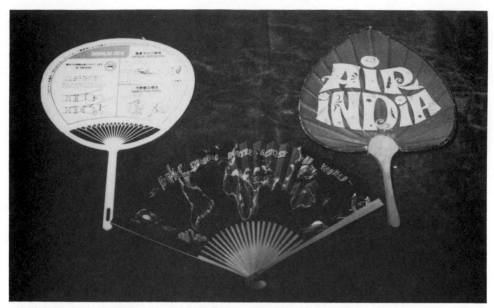

Fans are an unusual advertising giveaway, but at least 100 different varieties are known to exist. The one on the left is unusual in that it doubled as a DC-3 safety card; **$10** each. (From the Shirley and Larry Ibsen collection.)

Lighters were used as an advertising giveaway by many airlines over the years. Now that smoking is getting the blame for everything from hangnails to heart attacks, this form of advertising will probably disappear; **$15–$35** each. (From the Shirley and Larry Ibsen collection.)

Some of the many varieties of common mugs. **$5** each

United issued these attractive plaques to its frequent fliers. The wood shield was 8½" tall by 6½" wide; the metal is all polished brass. Plaques were issued to a passenger for having flown 100,000 miles on United. The one pictured also bears a "Million Miler" citation; the person who received this plaque must have spent many, many hours off the ground. Plain, **$30;** Million Miler, **$40.**

Paper-clip holder from tiny Air Illinois, a carrier no longer in existence. **$5**

Bright and colorful plastic baggage tags with a pocket in which to insert a business card. **$1–$3** each

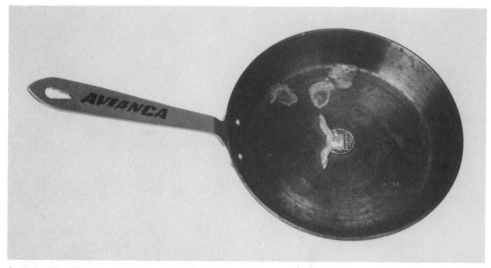

Small (5″ long) frypan ashtray from Avianca. **$5**

Coasters. The center two paper versions are from in-flight service, while the Mexicana (plastic) and Delta (metal) versions are gift shop or advertising giveaways. Paper, **25¢** each; metal or plastic, **$1** each.

Flight bags also came in miniature size; these are 7" wide by 4" high. Mohawk, **$10;** Ozark, **$5.**

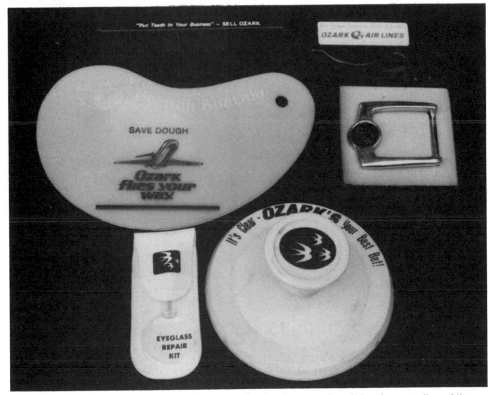

Even the relatively small Ozark Airlines cranked out a good variety of promotional items. Belt buckle, **$5;** other items, **$1** each.

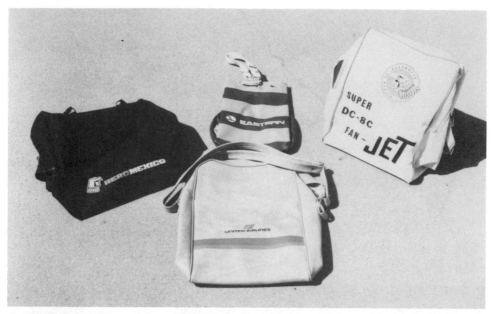

A few of the many varieties of flight bags that abound. Those which specify a plane model, such as the Aeronaves bag shown here, are especially desirable. Most varieties are **$5,** but if a bag is from a long-gone airline or specifies a plane type its value is **$10–$20.**

Silk-screen pennants from Brazil's Varig Airlines. Measuring about 6" × 12", these are especially attractive. One depicts a Constellation plane, and the other touts the Caravelle, an early jet. **$10** each

Lufthansa wall calendar with color painting of stewardess and young passenger. Image of Constellation aircraft at upper right. **$35**

TWA wall calendar with Constellation plane in color at the top of each month's page. **$25**

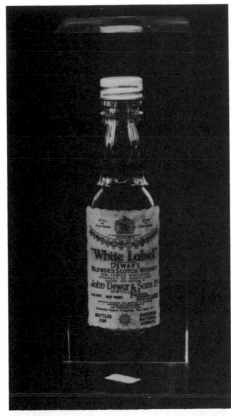

Scotch miniature inside a plastic cube, from Overseas National Airways. It may have been used as a paperweight. **$20**

One of the famous Airtray brand chrome plane ashtrays; the Airtray name is on the bottom of the base. This example is especially desirable as the plane it is modeled after is a rare prewar Boeing Stratoliner (only about eight were built). Other features make this collectible very valuable: propellers are intact; paint on plane and logo are in good condition; and chrome is in good condition. **$250**

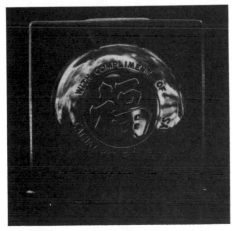

A small (3" diameter) oriental gong in brass was given out by Cathay Pacific, the famous and well-regarded airline of Hong Kong. **$7**

This Constellation plane model was probably used as a paper-clip holder. Eastern's name is on the pedestal, but the airplane model itself bears no airline markings. **$100**

An American DC-3 Airtray. **$200**

Ashtrays from Delta DC-4 (left) and Chicago & Southern Convair (right). Although not Airtray brand, these two are attractive and also somewhat rare. The Delta model has an old logo design, and C&S was a very small carrier; **$200—$225** each (From the John R. Joiner collection.)

Delta DC-7 travel agent model, made of metal. Example shown has minor wear; **$500.** If in mint condition, add 50 percent. (From the John R. Joiner collection.)

Ozark DC-9, the so-called travel agent model, made of plastic. **$200**

Capital Airlines Constellation ("Connie") travel agent model. This example has everything going for it: the airline and plane model are popular favorites; it is made of metal,
is in excellent condition, and has no missing parts; and it has an attractive chrome base
with both the airline name and plane model shown. It is hard to find one this good!
$2,000—$2,500. (From the Shirley and Larry Ibsen collection.)

Delta DC-9 travel agent model, made of metal. **$300** (From the John R. Joiner collection.)

Porcelain metal sign from the short period when both the Delta and C&S names were the actual corporate identity; **$100.** (From the John R. Joiner collection.)

Framed poster showing the various aircraft used by Western Airlines during its first 35 years; 11″ × 16″ size; **$35.** (From the John R. Joiner collection.)

Framed, hand-colored 8″ × 10″ lithograph of a Western Fokker Tri-Motor in flight. The frame is original; the paper backing is rubber-stamped "Western Air Express New York City." This is a rare example of a commercial aviation artifact from the 1920s. **$50**

These baggage labels are classified as scarce and command a price of about **$25** each (From the Hal Turin collection.)

These attractive labels are very common and are valued at **$3** each. (From the Hal Turin collection.)

These uncommon labels are valued at about **$10** each. (From the Hal Turin collection.)

This Panagra/Pan Am sticker is considered very scarce and is worth **$50.** (From the Hal Turin collection.)

9 Playing Cards

Although they could be classified as an advertising or in-flight item, playing cards constitute a major segment of the airline collectibles hobby all by themselves. Collected not only by a sizable portion of the aviation collector group, playing cards from airlines are collected widely by the many playing-card interest groups (usually called "societies") worldwide.

During nearly all of the years of commercial aviation history, playing cards have been used as a low-cost giveaway to passengers, something to while away their time during flights and provide promotion for the airline at the same time. The tradition continues to this day. Most of the world's major airlines still give away cards on their flights. A few airlines make a nominal charge for the cards, while others have different cards available free for first or business class or coach. Cards are a collectible that can be assembled into a nice display at minimal cost.

Today, there are approximately 1,700 different known airline card decks. Those seriously interested should obtain a copy of *Airline Playing Cards,* which, along with several supplements, illustrates every known deck. No pricing data is included in the publication, but the year of issue of many decks is shown, and a brief history of each airline is provided.

The earliest airline card decks date back to the late 1920s. One of the most famous is the 1929 deck issued by Transcontinental Air Transport (TAT), promoting the short-lived air/rail coast-to-coast service. Popular themes on the cards are destinations served by the airlines, as well as pictures or drawings of the aircraft. Delta issued a series of 12 decks featuring cities it served in 1959, then in 1969 issued a series of 24 and in 1975 another group of 12. Each of the three series has a unique graphic design. These decks are referred to as the "poster" series because the airline produced large posters for travel agencies and ticket offices with the same design as the cards. Delta is one of a handful of airlines which has issued over 50 different decks.

In the early 1970s TWA issued a collectors series of 16 different decks, each one depicting a type of plane which the airline operated and the year the plane was first used. The first one depicted was the Ford Tri-Motor of 1929 and the final one was the Lockheed L-1011 in 1972. These are a very popular series. Most of the decks in this series are valued in the $8–$10 range. Strangely, the last three decks issued are the hardest to find; the L-1011 is valued at $10. The two decks previous to the L-1011 were the 747, the only plane type depicted on two different decks (one deck shows the plane flying to the right, the other one shows it going left). These are the most scarce, costing $15 each.

As a general rule, the larger the airline, the more common the decks it has issued and thus the lower the prices for the decks. Also an evaluation factor is the length of time the particular deck design was distributed. American, Delta, TWA, and United had decks that were issued for a good many years; consequently, such decks are very common and are worth only $1. On the other hand, Russia's Aeroflot, easily the world's largest airline, has issued only a few different decks, which are very hard to obtain, and are worth approximately $100.

Some of the medium-size, now-defunct U.S. carriers rate special mention here due to the unusual value of their cards. The ''old'' Braniff (which went bankrupt and shut down in 1982) issued 11 different deck designs. The final two are very common ($2–$5), while all of the older examples are worth $25–$50. Three airlines are remembered fondly by former employees and passengers: Capital (which merged into United in 1961), Northeast (which merged into Delta in 1972), and Southern (which merged with North Central to form Republic in 1979). Each of these airlines issued several different decks, and every one of the different decks, although not exceedingly old, is relatively scarce, with a value of $35–$50 each.

A small and short-lived carrier was Air Atlanta, which had only about six planes and operated from approximately 1984 to 1986. Air Atlanta had four different card decks; each is worth $15–$20. But in 1989, several thousand decks of one design (bright yellow name and logo on a wine red background) were found in a warehouse. These decks have found their way to many flea market and airline show dealers, with the law of supply and demand driving the price down to about $5 per deck.

Most current decks, even for the obscure lines, go for $3–$7, with prices roughly doubling for each previous decade. The very early decks, such as the TAT airrail deck described above, are worth $200; most other prewar decks are worth $100–$125.

An early Continental deck. **$75**

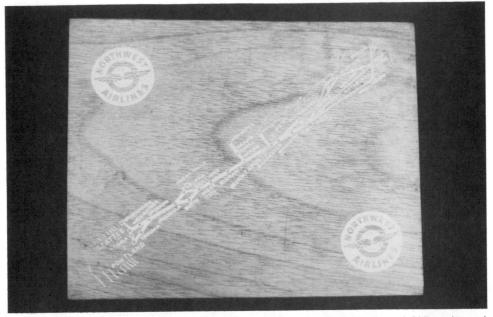

No, not a deck of cards, but the lid of a wooden box in which Northwest Airlines issued double card decks in the 1930s. The cards inside are worth **$50** a deck, and the box is valued at **$50** also.

An attractive card deck from Aeroflot, with gold markings on a black background; probably 10 to 15 years old. Trying to obtain cards from Aeroflot flights or offices brings the response that the airline doesn't have them and never did. **$100**

One of the Delta poster-series decks. **$5**

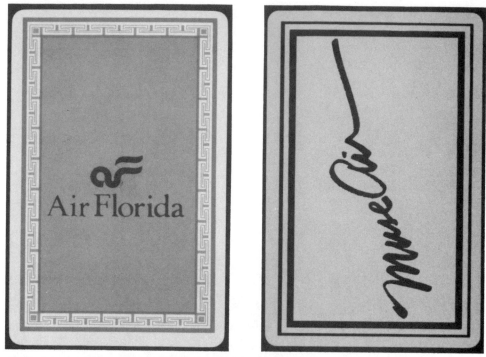

Air Florida and Muse Air cards. Each deck is only about 10 years old but is fairly scarce. **$10–$15**

Older decks from a few foreign carriers. **$20** each

Older decks from some of today's major carriers. **$30–$40** each

Three foreign decks. **$10** each

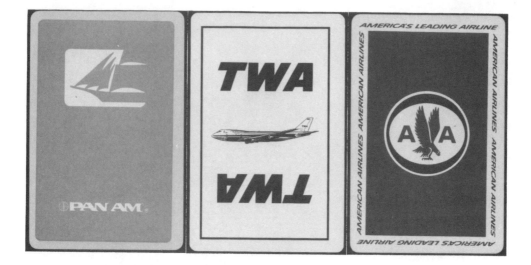

A variety of fairly common domestic and foreign decks. **$5** each

Three decks from the 1950s and 1960s that are fairly scarce. **$35** each

Some playing cards are round, including these two from Qantas and Thai Airways. Qantas, **$10;** Thai, **$15.**

One of the TWA Collector Series decks. All have the plane model and year on a black panel along the bottom. Deck pictured, **$8;** the L-1011 deck, **$10;** both 747 decks, **$15** each.

DOUGLAS DC-9 - 1966

Two small-size decks. BOAC, **$10;** Japan, **$5.**

Not to be confused with the Collector Series, these are other card decks issued by TWA in the early 1950s with color plane photos. They are scarce. **$35** each

Three very old and rare TWA decks. The TAT is from 1929, the DC-2 from 1934, and Stratoliner from 1940. **$150–$200** each

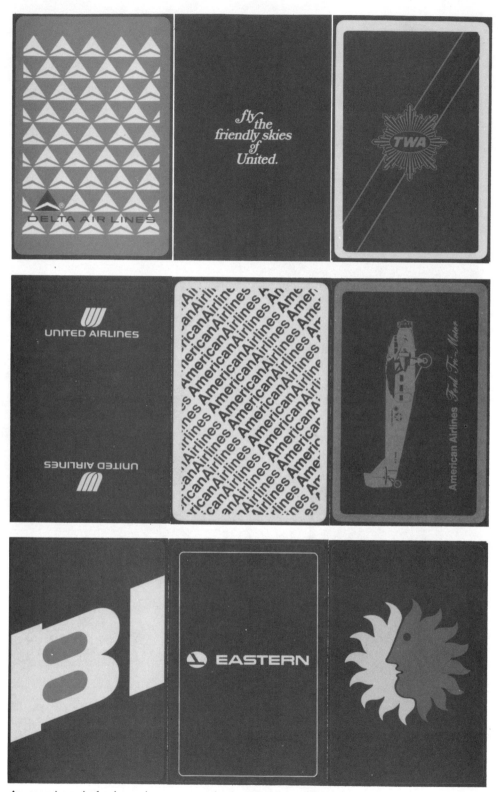

An assortment of extremely common decks, of which millions may have been distributed.
$1 each

10 Miscellaneous

Some airline collectibles do not fit into the other chapter categories because they do not meet the used by, issued by, or made for commercial airline criteria.

Books

Many thousands of books have been written about commercial aviation. Of the small number I have read, a few are worth special note here because of their exceptional quality. At the risk of overlooking other equally fine volumes, I will recommend a handful of books I believe would be useful and interesting to the collector.

Under the subject of history, there are a number of books authored by Robert J. Serling. Serling has done extensive research into airline corporate records, but more important, he has interviewed many retired employees who were active during the formative years of each airline. This is not a typically dry corporate history; each book is laced with interesting anecdotes about the colorful characters within each airline. The author's writing style nicely blends historical information with the persons who made the history, giving the background as to why decisions were made the way they were. While the volumes are meagerly illustrated, the text more than makes up for this shortcoming. Serling's airline history books include the following: *From the Captain to the Colonel* (Eastern Airlines), *Maverick* (Continental Airlines), *The Only Way to Fly* (Western Airlines), *Howard Hughes' Airline* (TWA), *Eagle* (American Airlines), and *Ceiling Unlimited* (North Central Airlines). Some may be out of print, but all are generally found at many of the airline shows; they are priced in the range of $15–$20.

Another fine series of history books has been produced by George W. Ccarley, Jr. These are paperback, about 100 pages each, but contain several hundred illustrations of planes, timetables, baggage labels, and other airline collectibles. Each has ample text on airline corporate history and the aircraft each airline owned. Among the airlines covered by this author to date are; American (two different books), Braniff (two different books), Capital, Delta, Eastern, National, TWA, and Western. Most are available at airline shows or from their author. Some may be out of print.

For those researching old airline names and dates of operation, *Airlines of the United States Since 1914* by R. E. G. Davies (Smithsonian

Press, 1972; reprinted 1982, 1984) will provide this information. A brief history is given of the larger lines, and the fate of every line is given, as to whether operations were discontinued or taken over by another company. This book is about 750 pages long and is moderately illustrated. It can be obtained from the publisher (about $40) or found at airline shows. Also from the same author: *A History of the World's Airlines* and *Airlines of Latin America Since 1919.*

Three large-format (9″ × 12″) paperback books have recently been issued by author Don Thomas. *Nostalgia Panamericana* is loaded with illustrations, most in color, of the flying boat era of Pan Am, as well as the world's other flying boat operators. Many rare timetables, folders, and baggage stickers are shown in the 65-page book. *Lindbergh and Commercial Aviation* shows many photographs, timetables, baggage stickers, etc., relating to Lindbergh's years as an adviser to TWA and Pan Am. Many excellent color plates are included in the approximately 40 pages. *Poster Art of the Airlines* depicts in full color many rare and beautiful travel posters from the world over, with perhaps a special emphasis on flying boats. Most are shown large, one to a page. About 65 pages. All three books are available from Don Thomas (1801 Oak Creek Dr., Dunedin, FL 34698) or at airline shows.

For those wishing to research early commercial airline operations, *Birth of an Industry* is an interesting volume put together by Reuben H. Donnelley, publishers of today's *Official Airline Guide*. The book contains reprints of 12 selected issues of the *Official Aviation Guides* from the years 1929–39, including the very first issue which came out in February 1929. Big and heavy (2″ thick; weight 6 pounds), this volume contains schedules, maps, lists of officers, and equipment descriptions that would be extremely difficult and expensive to assemble from timetables of the individual carriers. This book may be out of print and not easy to find. A used copy recently sold for about $60.

A handy small volume (5″ × 8″) for quick reference to more recent airlines is *The Airline Handbook,* by Paul K. Martin. Apparently no longer published, the final edition came out in 1985 or 1986. There have been 9 or 10 editions published over a period of about 12 years. Each of the world's airlines is listed in alphabetical order, showing logo, home office address, major cities and/or countries served, brief history, number of employees, list of aircraft owned or on order by type, and miscellaneous recent relevant information. In paperback, with some illustrations, the book is about 600 pages. Occasionally, used copies are available at airline shows for $15–20. This book contains a wealth of information in a small package.

For the serious plane-by-plane enthusiast, *jp airline-fleets international* is an annual paperback publication which details each of the world's airlines alphabetically by continent. Information in the book includes name and logo, home address, phone, number of employees, year of founding, and name of president for each airline. Every single aircraft operated by each airline is given its own listing, including its registration number, type, serial number, former registration (if any), year built, number and type of engines, maximum takeoff weight, configuration (freight or passenger; if the latter, how many coach/business/first class seats), and other miscellaneous information. The most recent edition has a section of 63 color photos of airliners. It is published by Bucher Publications, Switzerland, and is available at airline shows for about $35.

Copies of the *Official Airline Guide* make interesting reading for the airline enthusiast. Issued monthly since 1929, the *Guide* offers schedules for each airline and also lists classes of service offered, plane type, and meal service information, for each flight. Presently it is issued in North American and Worldwide editions, plus some pocket-size versions. An older copy can be a valuable research tool because it reports which airlines went where that month, how many flights a day there were, and what kind of craft was used.

In other words, one of these volumes is like having a complete time-table for every airline for that month. Older copies are scarce, and thus bring a good price: from the 1970s, $10; 1960s, $25; 1950s, $50; 1940s, $100.

Covers

Here we infringe a bit into the stamp-collecting hobby by discussing covers which have been around since the early days of commercial aviation as important collectibles. These items consist of a regular postal envelope with a special marking called a "cachet" on the left side denoting a particular event, such as a first flight or an anniversary of service on a particular route. Often the stamp bears a special cancellation. Many recently issued covers are valued in the $1 range, but rare items such as a cover of Pan Am's flying boat inaugural flights, signed by the crew, would be worth $100 or more. After Lindbergh's historic flight, he made a ceremonial trip on the St. Louis–Springfield–Peoria mail run that had been his regular job before his day of fame. So many requests were received for special "Lindbergh Flies the Mail Again" covers that several planes were needed to carry all the envelopes. Lindbergh flew each plane for a part of the route, so all covers could genuinely be items carried on a plane piloted by the hero. But there are so many of these that their value today is a relatively paltry $5.

Personalities

The airline industry has been shaped by many persons whose names were once household words, and the collection of items relating to these people is a legitimate part of the aviation collectibles hobby.

Orville and Wilbur Wright were not directly involved in any specific airline per se, but items directly related to the pair are sought by widely varied collector groups worldwide. In 1938, the Wright family home and bicycle shop were moved to Ford's Greenfield Village Museum at Dearborn, Michigan. A copy of the dedication program signed by Orville Wright was recently appraised at $1,400. Wilbur Wright items are much more scarce because he passed away in 1912.

Lindbergh, of course, was associated more with commercial airlines than any other single person. He was a consultant to TWA, which capitalized on his name by using the "Lindbergh Line" slogan on everything the company had at the time, including the planes. Later he was similarly employed by Pan Am and flew survey flights for the company in some of the very early flying boats. Because of his wide fame and long life, so many Lindbergh artifacts exist that the values are not as high as might be expected. A simple signature is worth $70, but a signed letter ranges from $500 to $800. Reputable autograph or manuscript dealers should be consulted regarding such items.

Nearly every sizable airline has been associated with an individual who founded or headed it for a long period of time. A few recognizable names are Eddie Rickenbacker (Eastern), Harris Hanshue (Western), Howard Hughes (TWA), Juan Trippe (Pan Am), C. E. Woolman (Delta), C. R. Smith (American), and Robert Six (Continental). Items relating to or signed by these persons range in value from $25 to $100, with Hughes items going somewhat higher as his fame transcended his involvement in TWA.

Lighter Than Air

The very first airships, of course, were the balloons, followed by dirigible-type craft which had their own power and steering mechanisms, rather than relying on wind currents. The German Zeppelins operated scheduled international passenger service for about 10 years; the 1937 timetable states that over 16,000 passengers had been carried by that point in time. The Graf Zeppelin was the veteran of the fleet. The Hindenburg's flaming death at Lakehurst, New Jersey, in 1937 was a tragedy of worldwide note that changed the course of aviation history. Although the Hindenburg made half a dozen routine round trips to the United States in 1936, the Hindenburg disaster brought a swift end to this fascinating era of air travel—the Graf Zeppelin was immediately retired.

Artifacts from both of these craft, although rare, do exist. China pieces are worth in the range of $750–$1,000 each. Timetables are valued in the $100–$200 range.

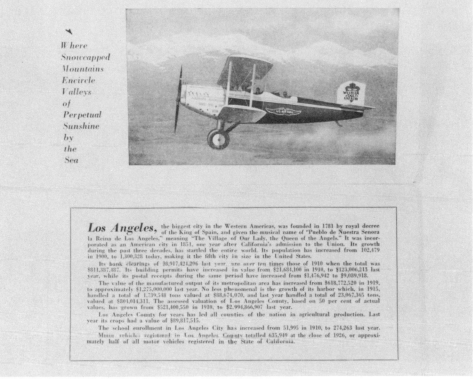

This fold-over card celebrated the first anniversary of one of the country's first and longest-lived carriers. The Douglas M-2 biplane is shown in maroon and gray. Passengers needed goggles and warm clothes in one of these! **$50**

Anniversary cover from American Airlines on the mail route which Lindbergh had inaugurated. **$10**

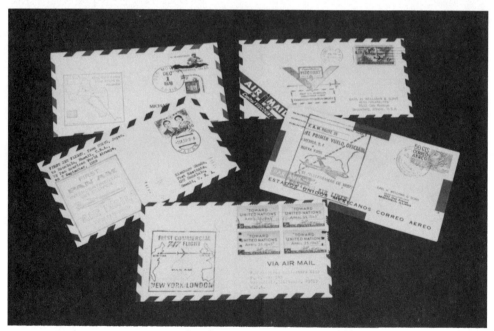

A sampling of first-flight covers. **$5—$10**

Pocket mirror with Pan Am flying boat on the reverse; probably not airline issue. **$5**

Tureen from the Graf Zeppelin, **$750;** dinner plate from the Hindenburg, **$900**

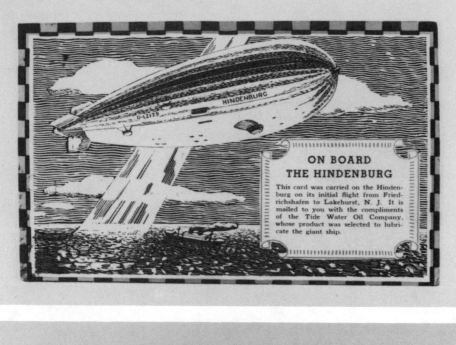

This historic postcard was carried on the initial trip of the Hindenburg in 1936. The 1936 season went fine, but on the first trip of 1937 the airship exploded. **$100**

Program from the dedication of the Wright family home and shop at Henry Ford's Greenfield Village in 1938. An otherwise interesting curio was made much more valuable by the signature of the guest of honor on the cover. **$1,400**

Postcards of the Hindenburg and Graf Zeppelin. **$35** each

Lufthansa poster (27″ × 41″) from the 1930s depicts Junkers trimotor and an earlier form of transport; **$950.** (From the Jon Simmonds collection.)

Russian Intourist poster (23″ × 36″) from 1934 depicts a Soviet aircraft of the era, with a route map; very rare; **$1,100.** (From the Jon Simmonds collection.)

Colonial Airlines poster (27″ × 41″) from the 1950s depicts a DC-4 flying over Bermuda; **$350.** (From the Jon Simmonds collection.)

KLM Royal Dutch Airlines poster (26″ × 39″) from 1931 showing a Fokker trimotor and the line's route from Amsterdam to Batavia (now Djakarta); **$950.** (From the Jon Simmonds collection.)

Lufthansa poster (25″ × 39″) from 1955 shows a pretty stewardess with a young passenger; **$275.** (From the Jon Simmonds collection.)

Pan American poster (27" × 41") from the 1930s is one of the most beautiful of the many flying-boat posters issued by Pan Am. The scene shows the Boeing 314 "Honolulu Clipper" at the dock after an overnight flight to Hawaii; **$950.** (From the Jon Simmonds collection.)

Appendixes

Genealogy of the Big Four, 1925–1930

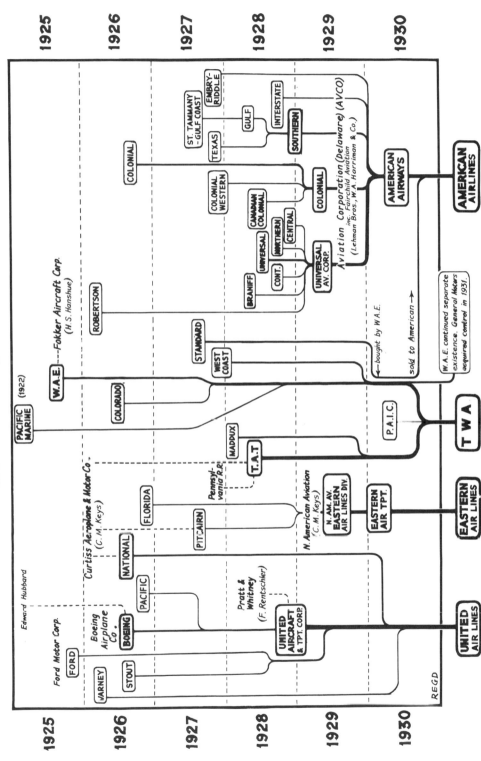

Courtesy of R. E. G. Davies.

1 Airline Names and Operating Dates

This section may help the collector identify, and possibly date, items from various large airlines. Generally the dates are taken from *The Airline Handbook,* and may possibly vary from other sources in that some dates listed here may document when service began rather than the year the airline was incorporated. Listings are in alphabetical order by the name or initials by which the airline is customarily known. TWA, for example is known more by its initials than by Trans World Airlines, while United is commonly referred to by that first word of its name, rather than by its initials, UAL.

Existing Airlines

In the interest of keeping this listing to a manageable size, current airline entries are limited to those carriers which operate 40 or more fixed-wing (i.e., non-helicopter) craft in passenger service. The listings are based on the 88/89 Edition of *jp airline-fleets international*. Although the listing includes a few large commuter or regional carriers, most of the listings are of large international airlines. Most collectibles originated from the larger airlines.

   The date following the name is the year in which the airline or its original predecessor was organized or started operations. Former names (f/n), if any, follow the date and show names and years in which those names were used. If the airline is the result of a consolidation of several predecessors at one time, the date shown is that of the consolidation, rather than of predecessors. Country of origin is shown in parentheses, unless it is obvious from the actual airline name.

Aeroflot Soviet Airlines, 1923; f/n Droblet, 1923–28; Drobflot, 1928–32

Aeromexico, 1934; f/n Aeronaves de Mexico, 1934–72

Air Algerie (Algeria), 1946; f/n Compagnie Generale de Transports Aeriens (CGTA), 1946–53

Air Canada, 1937; f/n Trans Canada Air Lines, 1937–64

Air France, 1933

Air Inter (France), 1954

Air Ontario (Canada), 1961; f/n Great Lakes Air Services/Great Lakes Airlines, 1961–81

Air Midwest (United States), 1965

Alaska Airlines, 1932; f/n McGee, 1932–34; Star Air Service/Star Airlines, 1934–42; Alaska Star Airlines, 1942–44

Alitalia (Italy), 1946; f/n Alitalie, 1946–57; LAI (Linee Aeree Italiane), 1946–57

All Nippon (Japan), 1952; f/n JHAT (Japan Helicopter and Airplane Transport Co.), 1952–58

American Airlines, 1930; f/n American Airways, 1930–34

America West, 1981

Ansett Airlines (Australia), 1936

Atlantic Southeast Airlines (ASA) (United States), 1979

Australian Airlines, 1946; f/n Trans Australian Airlines, 1946–85

Balkan-Bulgarian Airlines, 1947; f/n TABSO, 1947–68

Bar Harbor Airlines (United States), 1948

Braniff Airways (United States), 1928; f/n Paul R. Braniff, Inc., 1928–30; used the unofficial name Braniff International from about 1948–82; ceased operation 1982; re-started as Braniff Inc. 1984

British Airlines, 1972; f/n BOAC (British Overseas Airways Corp.), 1940–72; BEA (British European Airways), 1945–72

Britt Airways (United States), 1956; f/n Vercona Air Service

CAAC (Civil Air Administration of China), 1949; f/n CNAC (China National Aviation Corp.), 1949–54

Canadian Airlines International, 1942; f/n Canadian Pacific Airlines, 1942–68; CP Air, 1968–86

Comair (United States), 1977

Continental Airlines (United States), 1934; f/n Varney Speed Lines 1934; Varney Air Transport, 1934–37

CSA (Ceskoslovenske Aerolinie, Czechoslovakia), 1923

Cubana, 1930s (?)

Dan-Air London, 1953

Delta Airlines (United States), 1924; f/n Huff Daland Dusters, 1924–28; Delta Air Service, 1928–30 (operated as Delta/C&S Aviation, 1953–55)

Eastern Airlines, 1926; f/n Pitcairn Aviation, 1926–30; Eastern Air Transport, 1930–38

Finnair (Finland), 1923; f/n Aero O/Y 1923–46; Aero O/Y Finnish Air Lines, 1946–?

Garuda-Indonesian Airlines, 1950

Henson Airlines (United States), 1962; f/n Hagerstown Commuter

Horizon Air (United States), 1981

Iberia (Spain), 1940

Indian Airlines (India), 1953

Interflug (East Germany), 1953

Iraqi Airlines, 1945

JAL (Japan Airlines), 1951; f/n Japanese Airlines, 1951–53

Japan Air System, 1971; f/n TDA TOA Domestic Arline 1971–86

JAT (Jugoslovenski Aerotransport, Yugoslavia), 1947; f/n Aeroput, 1927–47

KLM-Royal Dutch Airlines (Netherlands), 1919

Korean Air, 1962; f/n Korean National Airlines, 1947–62; Korean Airlines, 1962–84

Libyan Arab Airlines, (1964) f/n Kingdom of Libya Airlines, 1964–69

LOT Polish Airlines (Polskie Linie Lotnicze), 1929

Lufthansa (Germany), 1926; f/n Deutsche Luft Hansa, 1926–54

MAS (Malaysian Airline System), 1947; f/n Malayan Airways; 1947–63; Malaysian Airways, 1963–66; Malaysian-Singapore Airlines, 1966–72

Mexicana, 1921

Midway Airlines (United States), 1979

Northwest Airlines (United States), 1926; f/n Northwest Airways, 1926–34, (used name Northwest Orient as a quasi-slogan, 1951–86)

Pakistan International Airways, 1951

Pan American World Airways, 1927; f/n Pan American Airways System, 1927–49

PBA (Provincetown-Boston Airlines, United States), 1949

Philippine Airlines, 1931; f/n Philippines Aerial Taxi, 1931–40

Qantas (Australia), 1920; f/n Queensland & Northern Territory Aerial Services, 1920–34; Qantas Empire Airways, 1934–67

SAS (Scandinavian Airlines System, Denmark/Norway/Sweden), 1946

Saudi Arabian Airlines, 1945

Simmons Airlines (United States), 1978

Singapore Airlines, 1972

Skywest Airlines (United States), 1972

South African Airways, 1934

Southwest Airlines (United States), 1967; f/n Air Southwest, 1967–71

Swissair, 1931

Talair (New Guinea), 1952; f/n Terrintory Airlines, 1952–75

TAROM (Transporturile Aeriene Romane, Romania), 1945; f/n TARS (Romanian-Soviet Air Transport, 1945–54

TAT French Regional Airlines, 1970

Thai Airways International, 1959

TWA (Trans World Airlines) (U.S.), 1926; f/n Transcontinental & Western Air, 1926–50 (merger of Western Air Express and TAT Maddux)

United Airlines (United States), 1931; 1931 merger of Boeing Air Transport, Pacific Air Transport, National Air Transport, and Varney Airlines

USAir, 1935; f/n All American Airways, 1937–53; Allegheny Airlines, 1953–79

Varig (Brazil), 1927

Westair Airlines (United States) Stol Air, 1972–83

Wings West Airlines (United States), 1979

Airlines of the Past

In this section, selected airlines have been included based on their size or historical significance. The fate of each airline listed is shown.

In this section, as well as in aviation research in general, there may be some confusion because of the large number of airlines with similar names. One in particular is the name "National," which seems to be one of the all-time favorite airline names. There was a National which merged into United in 1930, another which Pan Am acquired in 1980, plus an additional 10 existing today with National as the first word of their names (National Aeronautical Establishment, National Air Charter, National Air Charters, National Airlines, National Airways, National Executive Airlines, National Helicopters, National Jets, National Overseas Airline, and National Utility Helicopters). National Overseas Airline bears no relation to the National Airlines which formerly was named Overseas National Airways—clear as mud? Books described in Chapter 10, such as *jp airline-fleets international, The Airline Handbook,* and *Airlines of the United States Since 1914,* are invaluable in helping to identify many of the commonly found airline artifacts.

Air Atlanta, 1981; out of business 1986

AirCal, 1967; f/n Air California, 1967–81; into American Airlines, 1988

Air Florida, 1971; out of business 1984; assets to Midway

Allegheny, 1935; f/n All American Airways, 1937–53; name change to US Air 1979

British Caledonian, 1970; f/n Caldeonian/BUA, 1970–72; into British Airways, 1988

Capital Airlines, 1927; f/n Skyline Transportation, 1927–28; Pennsylvania Airlines, 1928–36; Pennsylvania-Central Airlines, 1936–48; into United Airlines, 1961

Chicago & Southern Air Lines, 1933; f/n Pacific Seaboard, 1933–35; into Delta Airlines, 1953

Colonial Airlines, 1928; f/n Canadian Colonial, 1928–42; into Eastern Airlines, 1956

Frontier Airlines, 1946; f/n Monarch Airlines, 1946–50; out of business 1986; assets to Continental

Imperial Airways Ltd., 1924; into British Overseas Airline Corporation, 1939

Jet America, 1981; into Alaska Airlines, 1986

Mid-Continent Airlines, 1928; f/n Hanfords Tri-State Airlines, 1928–38; into Braniff, 1952

Mohawk Airlines, 1945; f/n Robinson Airlines, 1945–52; into Allegheny Airlines, 1971

Muse Air 1981; acquired by Southwest Airlines 1986; operated under name Trans Star; out of business, 1987

National Airlines, 1934; into Pan American, 1980

North Central Airlines, 1948; f/n Wisconsin Central, 1948–52; merged with Southern to form Republic, 1979

Northeast Airlines, 1930; f/n Boston-Maine Airways, 1930–40; into Delta Airlines, 1972

Ozark Airlines, 1943; service gap 1945–50; into TWA, 1986

Pacific Northern Airlines, 1932; f/n Woodley Airways, 1932–47; into Western Airlines, 1967

PSA (Pacific Southwest Airlines, 1949); into USAir, 1988

Piedmont Airlines, 1948; into US Air, 1989

Regent Air, 1982; f/n Firstair, 1982–83; out of business, 1986

Republic Airlines, 1979 (by merger of North Central & Southern Airways); into Northwest, 1986

Southern Airways, 1949; merged with North Central to form Republic Airlines, 1979

Texas International, 1947; f/n Trans-Texas Airlines, 1947–68; into Continental Airlines, 1982

Transamerica Airlines, 1948; f/n Los Angeles Air Service, 1948–60; Trans International Airlines (TIA), 1960–79; out of business 1986

Trans Caribbean Airways, 1958; into American Airlines, 1971

Western Airlines, 1925; f/n Western Air Express, 1925–43 (was part of TWA, 1930–31); into Delta, 1987

Wien Airlines, 1924; f/n Wien Alaska, 1924–68; Wien Consolidated Airlines, 1968–73; Wien Air Alaska, 1973–84; out of business 1986

World Airways, 1948; out of business 1986

2 Airline Fleet Sizes

Historical Airline Fleet Sizes

Airline fleet sizes are listed in this section in an attempt to give some indication of comparable values of collectibles. The first chart is a tabulation of U.S. domestic airline fleet sizes from 1936 to 1969 which has been provided by R. E. G. Davies. All data is from the airlines' annual reports to stockholders.

	1936	1940	1945	1950	1955	1960	1965	1969
American	41	84	75	141	186	197	170	262
Braniff	13	9	12	28	58	61	60	73
Capital[1]	6	24	25	58	58	91		
Chicago & Southern[2]	3	8	6	17				
Colonial[3]	4	8	10	12	13			
Continental	4	14	6	15	29	32	27	54
Delta	4	8	19	32	56	87	88	139
Eastern	27	36	45	95	139	232	164	268
Inland[4]	4	4	4					
Mid Continent[5]	4	7	9					
National	4	5	12	28	38	45	40	56
Northeast	4	4	12	16	18	35	29	43
Northwest	14	14	22	51	47	58	64	119
Pan Am	28	56	93	138	120	158	116	164
TWA	28	42	58	138	167	186	171	231
United	47	56	67	139	176	205	292	358
Western	4	7	17	19	31	39	36	82

[1]part of United as of 1961; [2]part of Delta as of 1953; [3]part of Eastern as of 1956; [4]part of Western as of 1945; [5]part of Braniff as of 1952

Current Worldwide Fleet Sizes

The numbers shown below are based on entries in the 1988–89 edition of *jp airline-fleets international*, with the exception of the numbers for Aeroflot. Aeroflot is by far the world's largest airline, but quantifying the size of its commercial fleet is imprecise at best. Total aircraft operating under the Aeroflot name reportedly exceeds 10,000 entries, but this includes thousands of planes that are in government and military service. The best estimates of the portion of the Aeroflot fleet devoted to "public" commercial usage range from 2,500 to 3,000 craft. American Airlines was projecting to reach a fleet size of 600 by the end of 1989, to take away from United the title of the largest airline in the United States. Compared to Aeroflot, American's fleet is still tiny!

Aeroflot: 2,500–3,000 (see above)

Aeromexico: 45

Air Algerie: 55

Air Canada: 114

Air France: 140

Air Inter: 54

Air Midwest: 60

Air Ontario: 82

Alaska: 51

Alitalia: 86

All Nippon: 118

American: 506

America West: 84

Ansett: 65

Atlantic Southeast: 66

Austrailian: 57

Balkan-Bulgarian: 79

Bar Harbor: 74

Braniff: 52

British: 254

Britt: 47

CAAC: 300

Canadian: 99

Comair: 49

Continental: 371

CSA: 40

Cubana: 66

Dan-Air: 55

Delta: 464

Eastern: 284

Finnair: 57

Garuda-Indonesian: 83

Henson: 40

Horizon: 43

Iberia: 92

Indian: 63

Interflug: 58

Iraqi: 68

Japan/JAL: 107

Japan Air System: 91

JAT: 44

KLM: 76

Korean: 70

Libyan Arab: 60

LOT: 58

Lufthansa: 175

MAS: 48

Mexicana: 45

Midway: 51

Northwest: 277

Pakistan International: 40

Pan Am: 153

PBA: 61

Philippines: 49

Qantas: 40

SAS: 147

Saudia: 84

Simmons: 43

Singapore: 44

Skywest: 50

South African: 39

Southwest: 101

Swissair: 72

Talair: 56

TAROM: 92

TAT: 55

Thai: 46

TWA: 189

United: 434

USAir: 251

Varig: 81

Westair: 63

Wings West 56

3 Important Resources

The specific persons and/or publications listed below can be contacted to address any needs you may have in specific areas in connection with aviation collectibles. Many of the publications and persons listed here are seen frequently at airline collectible shows. Most of the persons listed here are involved in collecting only as a hobby in their spare time; thus, a stamped, self-addressed envelope is appreciated and will help speed a reply.

Major Hobby Organization: World Airline Historical Society, 3381 Apple Tree Lane, Erlanger, KY 41018. A quarterly publication, *Captain's Log,* has about 65 pages devoted to various aspects of the hobby and gives notice of show dates. The World Airline Historical Society acts as a sponsor of the organization's annual convention. The annual membership directory lists specific interests of each member. An active worldwide organization and a fine publication; membership dues $15.

Major Magazine: Airliners. In little more than a year, this new magazine has filled a niche in the hobby, featuring articles by and for the commercial airline enthusiast. About 65 pages, slick paper, with generous color use. Published quarterly from P.O. Box 52-1238, Miami, FL 33152-1238; annual subscription $14.95.

Airline History Books: George W. Cearley, Jr., P.O. Box 12312, Dallas, TX 75225. See "Books" section of Chapter 10 for titles; information on availability and price may be obtained by writing the author.

Airline Books, Calendars, Magazines, Models, Shirts, Slides, etc: AeroGem, Inc., 1224 N.W. 72nd Ave, Miami, FL 33152-1238. Write for listing of specific interests. Also operates a retail store called Just Plane Crazy at the same address.

Airline Playing Card Illustrated Guide Book: Fred Chan, Box 473, Burtonsville, MD 20866.

Airline Junior Wings Illustrated Guide Book: Stanley Baumwald, 2430 N.E. 35th St., Lighthouse Point, FL 33064.

Air Transport Label Illustrated Catalogs: Aeronautica and Air Label Collectors Club, P.O. Box 1239, Elgin, IL 60121.

Airline Collectibles General Information: The author of this book, Dick Wallin (P.O. Box 1784, Springfield, IL 62705), will try to answer questions and provide information on the buying or selling of specific items; or he will direct the inquiry to someone who can. Up-to-date information available on show locations and dates. Special interests and expertise: china, glassware, silver.

Playing Cards, Junior Wings, Travel Agent Models: Shirley and Larry Ibsen, 140 Springside Rd., Walnut Creek, CA 94596.

Crew Wings and Badges, Junior Wings, and Any Delta Airlines or Predecessor Items: John R. Joiner, 245 Ashland Trail, Tyrone, GA 30290.

Baggage Labels and Stickers, First Flight Covers, Postcards: Hal Turin, P.O. Box 158, San Dimas, CA 91773.

Airline Travel Posters: Jon Simmonds, 229 Beverly Rd., N.E., Atlanta, GA 30309.

Shows: At the time of this writing, the following information is timely: The "big" show, called Airliners International, is held annually in June or July, in a different location each year. The 1990 show will be held June 21–24 in Seattle, Washington; the 1991 show will be held in Orlando, Florida (dates to be announced). Typically, there are approximately 200 dealer tables. There are also regional shows, which have about 50 to 100 dealer tables. Locations of regional shows presently include Atlanta, Georgia (three per year); Newark, New Jersey; Miami, Florida (two per year); San Francisco, California (two per year); Los Angeles, California; Phoenix, Arizona; and Dallas-Ft Worth, Texas. Several former railroadiana shows are now being billed as transportation shows, to encourage the inclusion of airline, steamship, and bus items.

Index